MathFlare

Name: _______________________

Class: __________

Teacher: _______________________

Copyright © 2024 MathFlare Publishing.
All rights reserved. This book or any portion thereof may not be reproduced or used in any manner whatsoever without the express written permission of the publisher except for the use of brief quotations in a book review.

Introduction

As parents and educators, we recognize the pivotal role mathematics plays in shaping a child's academic journey and future success. Yet, the path to mathematical proficiency can often seem daunting, fraught with challenges and complexities. That's where the transformative power of MathFlare Workbooks shine through, illuminating the way forward with clarity, precision, and purpose.

Introducing MathFlare Workbooks – a beacon of guidance, a testament to excellence, and a catalyst for achievement. Crafted with meticulous care and expertise, MathFlare Workbooks stand as paragons of educational excellence, designed to nurture young minds, ignite a passion for learning, and develop a deep-rooted understanding of mathematical concepts.

Picture this: your child eagerly delves into the pages of Mathflare Workbook, greeted by a step-by-step guide illuminated with vivid examples that demystify complex mathematical concepts. With each turn of the page, they embark on a journey of discovery, encountering thoughtfully curated practice questions that reinforce learning and hone problem-solving skills. And when they unveil the answers to those very questions, a sense of accomplishment blossoms within them – a tangible reward for their hard work and dedication.

But MathFlare Workbooks are more than just tools for learning; they are pathways to comprehension, fostering a deep-seated understanding of mathematical concepts through a sequential, logical flow. From fundamental principles to advanced problem-solving strategies, every chapter builds upon the last, ensuring a robust foundation upon which future knowledge can be constructed.

As parents, we yearn for nothing more than to see our children thrive, to witness the spark of inspiration ignited within them as they conquer academic challenges with confidence and poise. MathFlare Workbooks serve as partners in this noble endeavor, offering not just practice questions, but the keys to unlocking a world of opportunity.

And for teachers, MathFlare Workbooks stand as invaluable allies in the quest to cultivate mathematical proficiency in the classroom. With answers readily available, instructors can focus on guiding and nurturing their students, confident in the knowledge that MathFlare Workbooks provide a solid framework upon which to build.

In the pages of MathFlare Workbooks, we find not just the promise of academic excellence, but the seeds of a brighter tomorrow. So let us embrace the power of mathematics, let us champion the journey of learning, and let us pave the way for a generation of young minds poised to shape the world. With MathFlare Workbooks as our guide, the possibilities are infinite, and the future, bright.

Table of Contents

Pre-Algebra	
Place Value	1
Operations with Whole Numbers	8
Operations with Decimals	18
Exponents	31
Square and Cube Roots	36
Multiple Operations with Fractions	41
Convert Ratios, Fractions, Percents, Decimals	51
Solving One-Step Equations	56

MathFlare
Grade 2
MATH WORKBOOK
Step by Step Guide and Essential Practice with Answers
Addition Subtraction
Multiplication
Place Value and Expanded Notations
Geometry
MathFlare Publishing

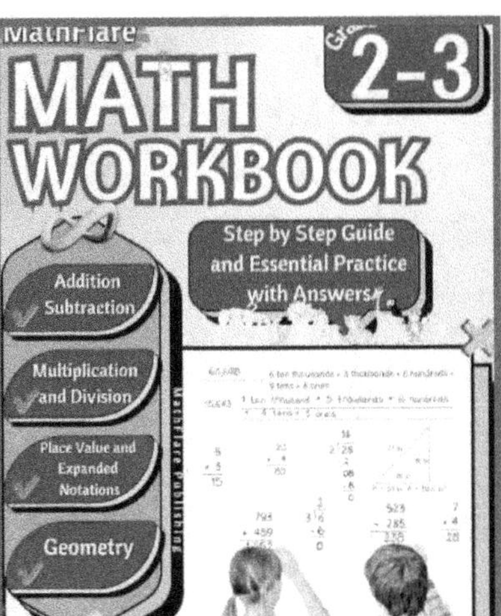
MathFlare
Grade 2-3
MATH WORKBOOK
Step by Step Guide and Essential Practice with Answers
Addition Subtraction
Multiplication and Division
Place Value and Expanded Notations
Geometry
MathFlare Publishing

MathFlare
Grade 3
MATH WORKBOOK
Step by Step Guide and Essential Practice with Answers
Multiplication and Division
Decimals
Place Value and Expanded Notations
Fractions and Geometry
MathFlare Publishing

MathFlare
Grade 1
MATH WORKBOOK
Step by Step Guide and Essential Practice with Answers
Counting and Numbers
Addition and Subtraction
Place Value and Expanded Notations
Understanding Time
MathFlare Publishing

MathFlare
Grade 1-2
MATH WORKBOOK
Step by Step Guide and Essential Practice with Answers
Counting and Numbers
Addition and Subtraction
Place Value and Expanded Notations
Understanding Time
MathFlare Publishing

MathFlare
Grade 3-4
MATH WORKBOOK
Step by Step Guide and Essential Practice with Answers
Addition Subtraction
Multiplication Division
Place Value and Expanded Notations
Fractions and Geometry
MathFlare Publishing

MathFlare
Grade 4
MATH WORKBOOK
Step by Step Guide and Essential Practice with Answers
Addition Subtraction
Multiplication Division
Place Value and Expanded Notations
Fractions and Geometry
MathFlare Publishing

MathFlare
Grade 4-5
MATH WORKBOOK
Step by Step Guide and Essential Practice with Answers
Multiplication Division
Place Value and Expanded Notations
Fractions and Geometry
Unit Conversion
MathFlare Publishing

MathFlare
Grade 5
MATH
WORKBOOK
Step by Step Guide
and Essential Practice
with Answers
Multiplication Division
Place Value and Expanded Notations
Fractions and Geometry
Unit Conversion
MathFlare Publishing

MathFlare
Grade 5-6
MATH
WORKBOOK
Step by Step Guide
and Essential Practice
with Answers
Multiplication Division
Place Value and Expanded Notations
Fractions and Geometry
Units and Statistics
MathFlare Publishing

MathFlare
Grade 6
MATH
WORKBOOK
Step by Step Guide
and Essential Practice
with Answers
Integers and Statistics
Arithmetic and Pre-Algebra
Fractions and Geometry
Ratio and Percentage
MathFlare Publishing

MathFlare
Grade 6-7
MATH
WORKBOOK
Step by Step Guide
and Essential Practice
with Answers
Arithmetic and Pre-Algebra
Ratio, Percent Proportion
Geometry
Statistics
MathFlare Publishing

MathFlare
Grade 7
MATH
WORKBOOK
Step by Step Guide
and Essential Practice
with Answers
Pre-Algebra
Ratio, Percent Proportion
Geometry
Statistics
MathFlare Publishing

MathFlare
Grade 7-8
MATH
WORKBOOK
Step by Step Guide
and Essential Practice
with Answers
Pre-Algebra
Ratio, Percent Proportion
Geometry and Cartesian Plane
Statistics
MathFlare Publishing

MathFlare
Grade 8-9
MATH
WORKBOOK
Step by Step Guide
and Essential Practice
with Answers
Pre-Algebra
Ratio, Proportion and Percentage
Linear Equations
Geometry and Cartesian Plane
MathFlare Publishing

MathFlare
Grade 8
MATH
WORKBOOK
Step by Step Guide
and Essential Practice
with Answers
Pre-Algebra
Percentage
Linear Equations
Geometry
MathFlare Publishing

Operations with Whole Numbers

Positive and negative integers are whole numbers that can represent quantities greater than zero and less than zero, respectively.

Positive Integers: Positive integers are whole numbers greater than zero. They are denoted by the numbers 1,2,3,4...

Negative Integers: Negative integers are whole numbers less than zero. They are denoted by placing a negative sign ("-") before the numbers, such as $-1, -2, -3, -4, ...$

The positive integers are used to represent the number of objects, scores, etc. whereas the negative integers can be used to represent debt, losses, temperatures below freezing points, etc.

Let's solve some problems:

1. $6 - (-8) - 9$

- Start by simplifying within the parentheses:

$$-(-8) \text{ becomes } 8.$$

- Rewrite the expression with the simplified part:

$$6 + 8 - 9.$$

- Now perform addition and subtraction from left to right:

$$6 + 8 = 14, \text{ then } 14 - 9 = 5$$

2. $(-5) - (-3) + 10$

$$(-5) + 3 + 10$$

$$(-5) + 3 = -2, \text{ then } -2 + 10 = 8$$

Operations with Decimals

Adding Decimals

Adding decimals is like adding whole numbers, but we must align the decimal points carefully. For instance, when adding 49.88 and 45.78:

Step 1: Align the decimal points.

$$
\begin{array}{r}
49.88 \\
+\ 45.78 \\
\hline
\end{array}
$$

Step 2: Start adding from the rightmost digit (the ones place) and move to the left.

Add 8 and 8: 8 + 8 = 16. Write down 6 in the ones place and carry over 1 to the tenths place.

$$
\begin{array}{r}
49.88 \\
+\ 45.78 \\
\hline
6
\end{array}
$$

Step 3: Add the tenths place.

Add 1 (carried over from the previous step), 8, and 7: 1 + 8 + 7 = 16. Write down 6 in the tenths place and carry over 1 to the hundredths place.

$$
\begin{array}{r}
49.88 \\
+\ 45.78 \\
\hline
66
\end{array}
$$

Step 4: Continue adding digits to the left until you reach the leftmost digit:

$$
\begin{array}{r}
49.88 \\
+\ 45.78 \\
\hline
9566
\end{array}
$$

<u>Step 5: Finally, write the sum with the decimal point directly below the decimal points in the original numbers.</u>

$$
\begin{array}{r}
49.88 \\
+\ 45.78 \\
\hline
95.66
\end{array}
$$

Let's solve a problem:

$$
\begin{array}{r}
835.68 \\
+\ 825.29 \\
\hline
1{,}660.97
\end{array}
$$

Subtracting Decimals

Subtracting decimals follows a process like adding decimals, except instead of adding the numbers, we subtract them.

For example:

$$
\begin{array}{r}
697.05 \\
-\ 258.40 \\
\hline
438.65
\end{array}
$$

Multiplying Decimals

Multiplying decimals is a lot like multiplying whole numbers, but we need to be careful about where we put the decimal point in the answer.

   Step 1: Start by multiplying the numbers together, just like we do with whole numbers. Ignore the decimals for now.

   Step 2: Count how many decimal places there are in the numbers we're multiplying. This will tell us how many decimal places our answer should have.

Step 3: Put the decimal point in the answer by starting from the right side of the number. Move the decimal point to the left as many places as there are in the total number of decimal places.

For example, let's multiply 4.5 by 2.5:

Step 1: Multiply the numbers as if they were whole numbers:

$$25 \times 45 = 1125.$$

Step 2: There is one decimal place in 2.5 and one in 4.5, making a total of two decimal places.

Step 3: Starting from the right side of the answer, count two places to the left and put the decimal point there.

So, the final answer is 11.25.

Remember to pay close attention to where the decimal point goes in the answer.

Let's solve a problem:

$$
\begin{array}{r}
85.39 \\
\times \quad 1.44 \\
\hline
+ \ 34156 \\
+ \ 34156 \\
+ \ 8539 \\
\hline
= 122.9616
\end{array}
$$

Dividing Decimals

Dividing decimals is a lot like dividing whole numbers, but we need to be careful about placement of decimal point in the answer.

Steps to follow:

1. **Set up the division problem:** Write the dividend (the number being divided) and the divisor (the number you're dividing by) as you would in a long division problem.

$$1.7 \overline{)1.6}$$

2. **Move the decimal:** Move the decimal point to the right in the dividend and divisor by the same number of places.

$$17 \overline{)16}$$

3. **Perform the division:** Divide as you would with whole numbers.

$$
\begin{array}{r}
0\,0.9\,4 \\
17 \overline{)16} \\
-0 \\
\hline
1\,6 \\
-0 \\
\hline
1\,6\,0 \\
-1\,5\,3 \\
\hline
7\,0 \\
-6\,8 \\
\hline
2
\end{array}
$$

4. **Place the decimal point:** Place the decimal point in the quotient directly above its position in the dividend.

So, the quotient is 0.94.

Let's solve another problem:

$$
\begin{array}{r}
4.567 \\
12\overline{)54.8} \\
-0 \\
\hline
54 \\
-48 \\
\hline
68 \\
-60 \\
\hline
80 \\
-72 \\
\hline
80 \\
-72 \\
\hline
8
\end{array}
$$

Using the Power of 10

Using the powers of 10, 100, and 1000 makes multiplying and dividing by these numbers very convenient. Let's illustrate with examples:

Multiplying by Powers of 10:

- To multiply a number by 10, simply move the decimal point one place to the right.

$$5 \times 10 = 50$$

- To multiply a number by 100, move the decimal point two places to the right.

$$5 \times 100 = 500$$

- To multiply a number by 1000, move the decimal point three places to the right.

$$5 \times 1000 = 5000.$$

Dividing by Powers of 10:

- To divide a number by 10, simply move the decimal point one place to the left.

$$50 \div 10 = 5$$

- To divide a number by 100, move the decimal point two places to the left.

$$500 \div 100 = 5$$

- To divide a number by 1000, move the decimal point three places to the left.

$$5000 \div 1000 = 5$$

Exponents and Roots

Exponents

An exponent tells us how many times a number (called the base) is multiplied by itself. It is written as a superscript to the right of the base number. For example, in 2^3, 2 is the base and 3 is the exponent.

Rules:

1. **Product Rule**: When multiplying powers with the same base, add the exponents.

$$a^m \times a^n = a^{m+n}$$

For example:

$$2^3 = 2 \times 2 \times 2 = 8$$

$$3^2 \times 3^4 = 3^{2+4} = 3^6 = 3 \times 3 \times 3 \times 3 \times 3 \times 3 = 729$$

2. **Quotient Rule**: When dividing powers with the same base, subtract the exponents.

$$a^m \div a^n = a^{m-n}$$

For example:

$$5^3 \div 5^2 = 5^{3-2} = 5^1 = 5$$

3. **Power of a Power Rule**: When raising a power to another power, multiply the exponents.

$$(a^m)^n = a^{mn}$$

For example:

$$(2^2)^3 = 2^{2 \times 3} = 2^6 = 64$$

4. **Power of a Product Rule:** When raising a product to a power, distribute the power to each factor.

$$(ab)^n = a^n \times b^n$$

For example:

$$(2 \times 3)^2 = 2^2 \times 3^2 = 4 \times 9 = 36$$

5. **Power of a Quotient Rule:** When raising a quotient to a power, distribute the power to the numerator and denominator separately.

$$\left(\frac{a}{b}\right)^n = \frac{a^n}{b^n}$$

For example:

$$\left(\frac{4}{2}\right)^3 = \frac{4^3}{2^3} = \frac{64}{8} = 8$$

6. **Zero Exponent Rule:** Any nonzero number raised to the power of zero equals 11.

$$a^0 = 1$$

For example:

$$7^0 = 1$$

7. **Negative Exponent Rule:** A negative exponent means the reciprocal of the base raised to the positive exponent.

$$a^{-n} = \frac{1}{a^n}$$

For example:

$$2^{-3} = \frac{1}{2^3} = \frac{1}{8}$$

To evaluate expressions with exponents, we can use:

- **Repeated Multiplication**: Perform the multiplication indicated by the exponent.

- **Using the Rules of Exponents**: Apply the appropriate rule to simplify expressions involving exponents.

Square Roots

The square root of a number is a value that, when multiplied by itself, gives the original number. It's denoted by the symbol $\sqrt{}$.

For example, the square root of 9 is 3 because 3 * 3 = 9.

Cube Roots

The cube root of a number is a value that, when multiplied by itself twice, gives the original number. It's denoted by the symbol $\sqrt[3]{}$.

For example, the cube root of 8 is 2 because 2 * 2 * 2 = 8.

Multiple Operations Fractions

Fraction multiple operations involve performing multiple arithmetic operations (addition, subtraction, multiplication, division) on fractions.

We follow (PEDMAS that stands for the order of operations in arithmetic) to solve multiple operations Fractions:

1. **Parentheses:** Perform operations inside parentheses first.

2. **Exponents:** Evaluate expressions with exponents or powers.

3. **Multiplication and Division:** Perform multiplication and division from left to right.

4. **Addition and Subtraction:** Perform addition and subtraction from left to right.

For example:

Let's solve the expression: $\dfrac{3}{4} + \dfrac{1}{2} \times \dfrac{2}{3}$

Step 1: Begin by performing the multiplication operation first:

$$= \frac{1 \times 2}{2 \times 4} = \frac{2}{6} = \frac{1}{3}$$

Step 2: Now rewrite the expression with the result of the multiplication:

$$\frac{3}{4} + \frac{1}{3}$$

Step 3: To add fractions, find a common denominator. In this case, the least common multiple (LCM) of 4 and 3 is 12.

Step 4: Rewrite both fractions with the common denominator:

$$\frac{9}{12} + \frac{4}{12}$$

Step 5: Add the numerators together and keep the common denominator:

$$\frac{13}{12} = 1\frac{1}{12}$$

Solving One-Step Equations

Solving one-step equations involves finding the value of the variable that makes the equation true. In a one-step equation, there is only one operation (addition, subtraction, multiplication, or division) performed on the variable.

The goal is to isolate the variable on one side of the equation by performing inverse operations.

For example:

Given the equation $6 = -3z$, where we want to solve for z.

The given equation is already in the form of a one-step equation, with z being multiplied by -3.

To isolate z, we need to perform the inverse operation of multiplication, which is division.

Divide both sides by -3:

$$\frac{6}{-3} = \frac{-3z}{-3}$$

Simplify:

$$-2 = z$$

So, the solution to the equation is $z = -2$.

When we substitute the value of $z = -2$ back into the original equation, $6 = -3(-2)$, it simplifies to $6 = 6$. This confirms that our solution is correct because it satisfies the original equation.

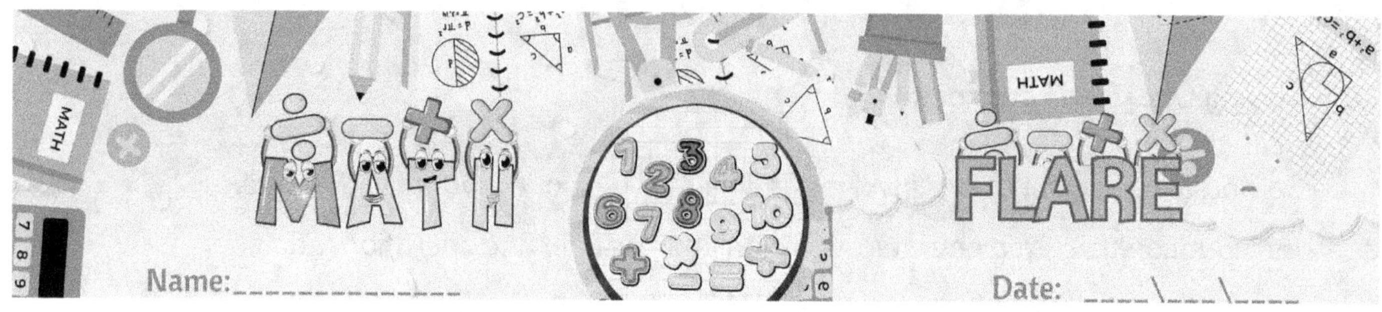

Place Value

Determine the place value of the underlined digit.

1. 15,123,884,652 = _______________________________

2. 33,979,096,754 = _______________________________

3. 81,927,134.455 = _______________________________

4. 986,155,196.03 = _______________________________

5. 493,229.28827 = _______________________________

6. 1,614,928,268.2 = _______________________________

7. 1,587,341,622.7 = _______________________________

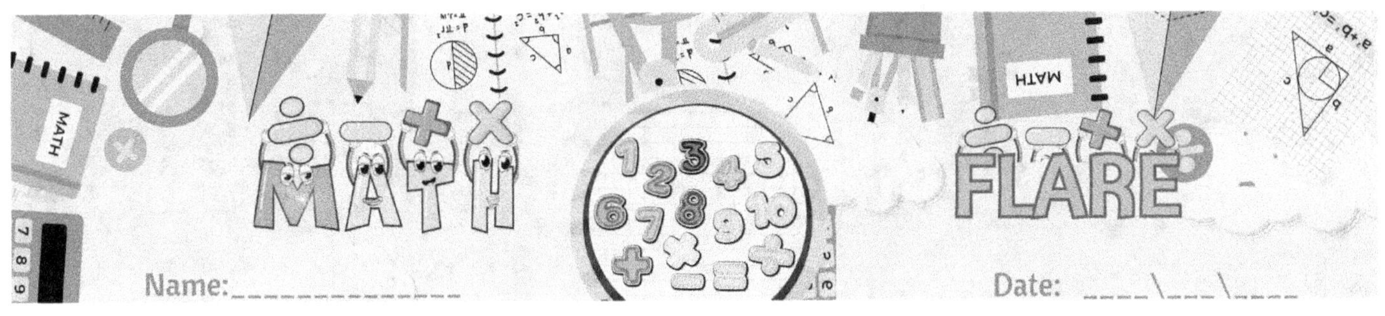

8. 2,550,447.9713 = _______________________

9. 214,784.51165 = _______________________

10. 8,294,578,304.1 = _______________________

11. 26,679,657.365 = _______________________

12. 12,027,774,198 = _______________________

13. 90,540,077,583 = _______________________

14. 955,934.44236 = _______________________

15. 783,147.4583 = _______________________

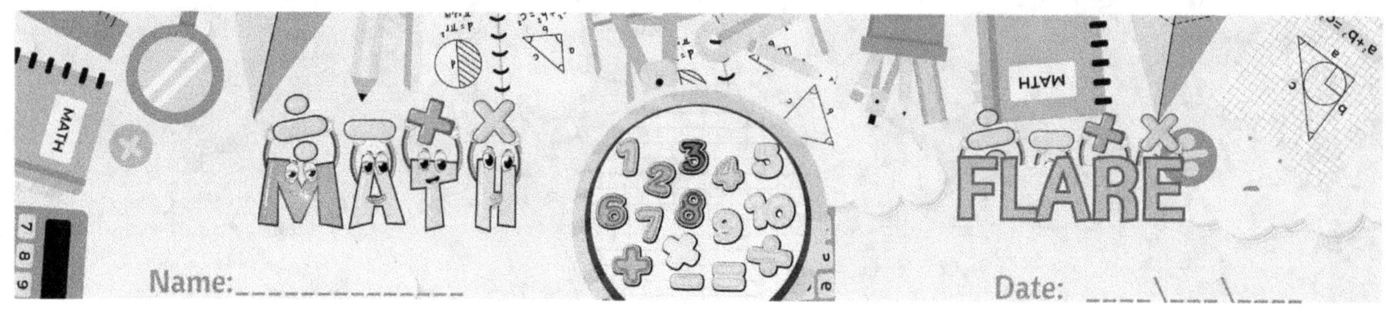

16. 8,887,969.749<u>8</u> = _______________________________

17. 7,631,385.<u>5</u>161 = _______________________________

18. <u>5</u>98,610,311.65 = _______________________________

19. 905,1<u>1</u>9.2277 = _______________________________

20. 252,603.4940<u>7</u> = _______________________________

21. 8,022,56<u>7</u>.0807 = _______________________________

22. 999,<u>9</u>16.59586 = _______________________________

23. 20,<u>9</u>40,326.611 = _______________________________

24. 818,386.27132 = _______________________________________

25. 81,733,519,323 = _______________________________________

26. 260,735.4929 = _______________________________________

27. 933,876,846.83 = _______________________________________

28. 36,960,029.172 = _______________________________________

29. 156,937.73225 = _______________________________________

30. 12,070,209.133 = _______________________________________

31. 77,842,603.156 = _______________________________________

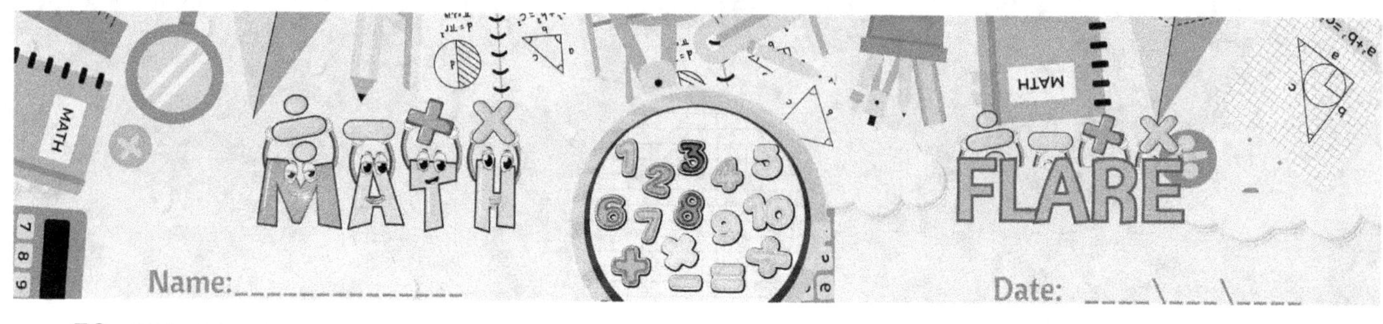

32. 35,601,972,097 = ___________________________

33. 47,098,044,914 = ___________________________

34. 2,918,575.304 = ___________________________

35. 95,152,901.589 = ___________________________

36. 87,324,687,576 = ___________________________

37. 35,487,901.058 = ___________________________

38. 790,981,071.85 = ___________________________

39. 499,105.75845 = ___________________________

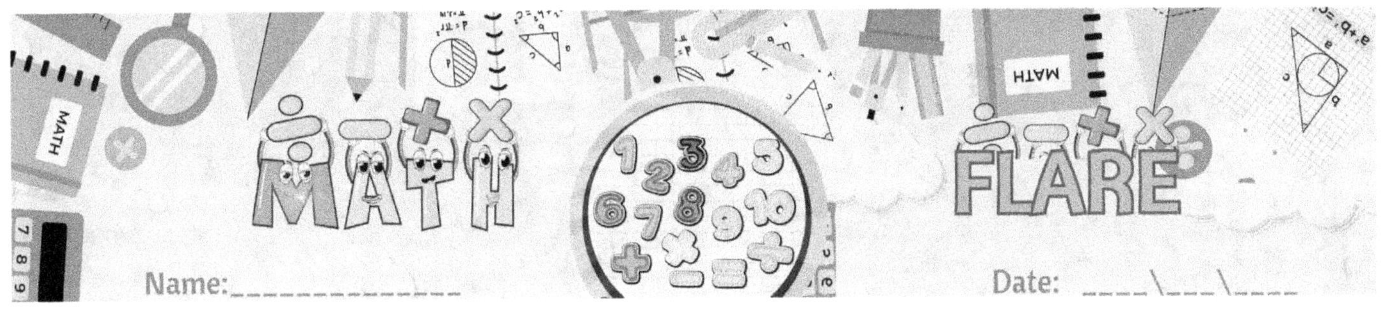

40. 6,027,109.1805 = _______________________________

41. 69,987,413,245 = _______________________________

42. 41,519,148.313 = _______________________________

43. 114,542,273.86 = _______________________________

44. 424,923.28846 = _______________________________

45. 8,145,387.8917 = _______________________________

46. 38,096,685,650 = _______________________________

47. 297,371,647.55 = _______________________________

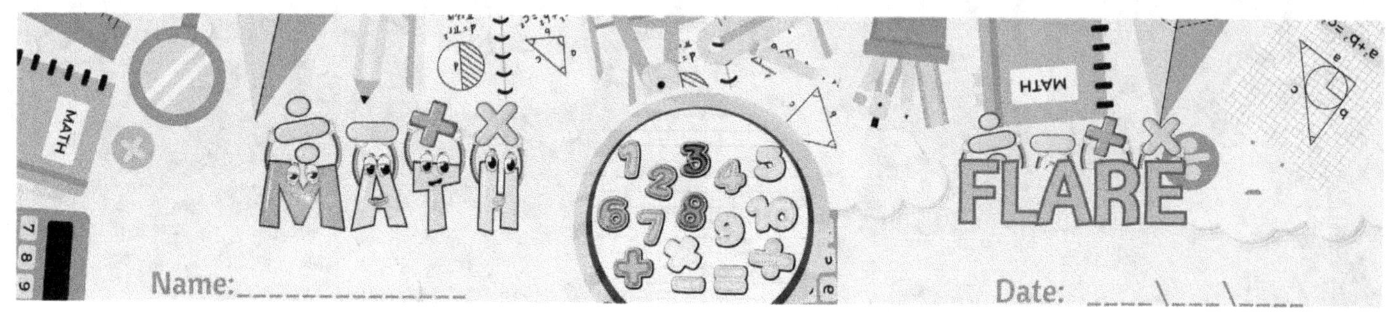

48. 418,591.77608 = _______________________________

49. 970,560,134.18 = _______________________________

50. 85,682,808.698 = _______________________________

51. 3,566,569,668.9 = _______________________________

52. 584,228.85801 = _______________________________

53. 35,025,415.385 = _______________________________

54. 321,474.29502 = _______________________________

55. 117,822,000.67 = _______________________________

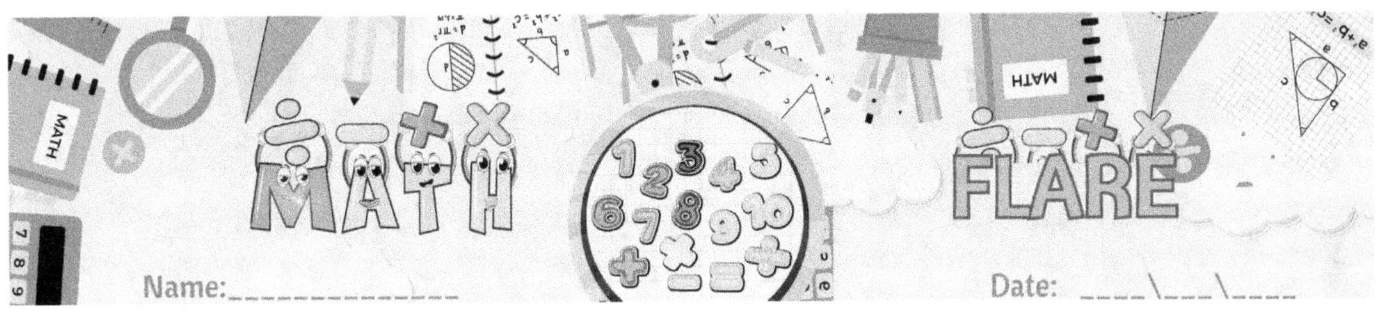

Operations with Whole Numbers

1. $5 - 7 + 10 =$

2. $4 - (2 + 1) - 5 =$

3. $3 + 7 - 2 =$

4. $7 - (3 - 5) =$

5. $9 - (-6) - 8 =$

6. $10 + (4 - 9) =$

7. $3 + 9 - (6 + 1) =$

8. $5 - 2 + 7 =$

9. $(-2) + (-5) + 5 =$

10. $4 - (3 + 1) + 10 =$

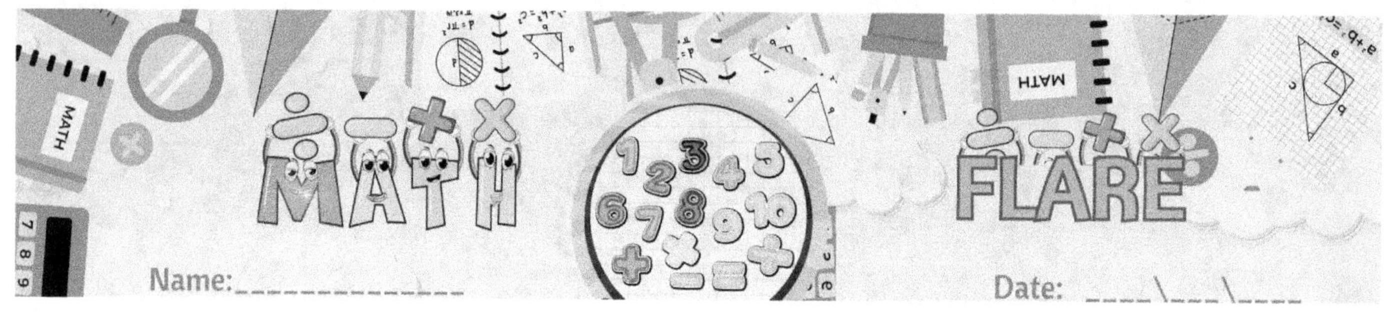

11. $6 + 7 - 4 =$

12. $10 + (5 - 8) =$

13. $7 - 8 - 6 - 10 =$

14. $6 - (7 + 3) - 5 =$

15. $10 - 7 - (3 + 7) =$

16. $4 + (-6) =$

17. $1 - (-3) =$

18. $9 + (-6) - 6 =$

19. $2 - (-6) =$

20. $9 + 1 - 8 =$

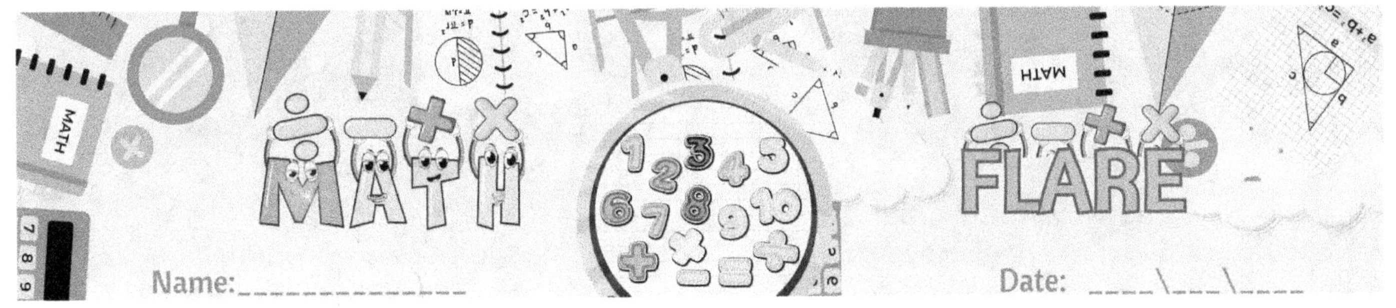

21. $4 + (-10) - 7 =$

22. $3 - (9 + 3) - 3 =$

23. $(-8) + (-6) + 6 =$

24. $2 - (-6) - 4 =$

25. $(-7) + (-6) + 9 =$

26. $10 - 2 - 3 =$

27. $8 - 3 + 7 =$

28. $9 - 5 + 9 =$

29. $4 + 8 - (8 + 4) =$

30. $3 + 3 - 9 + 7 =$

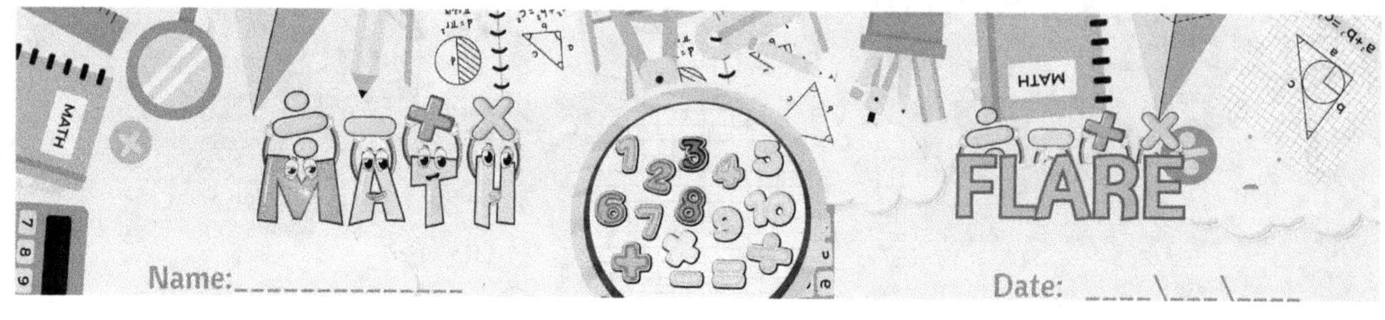

31. $8 + (6 - 6) =$

32. $10 + 10 - 6 =$

33. $7 + 5 - 5 =$

34. $1 - 8 + (- 4) =$

35. $6 + (10 - 3) =$

36. $1 - 8 + 3 =$

37. $4 + 7 - (3 + 6) =$

38. $7 - 1 - (3 + 4) =$

39. $6 - (6 + 6) + 5 =$

40. $(- 3) + 4 + (- 4) =$

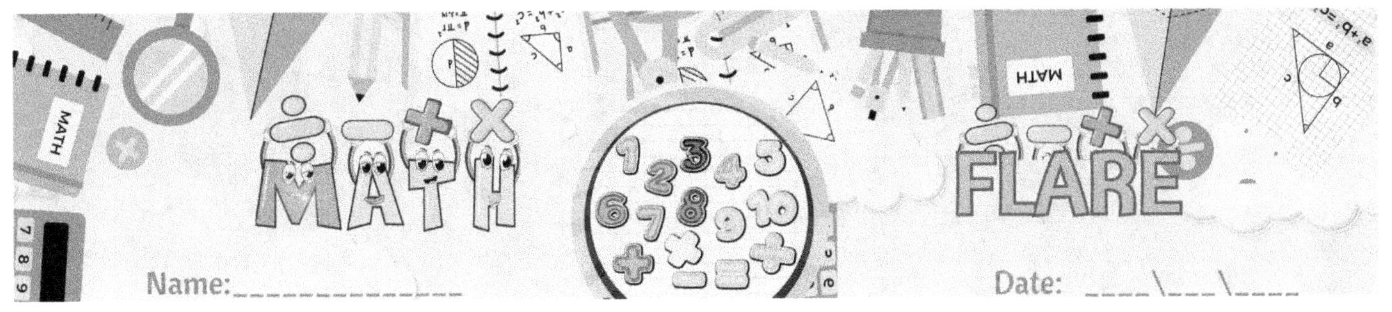

41. $(-9) + 7 + (-2) =$

42. $10 + (9 - 10) =$

43. $6 - 6 + 4 =$

44. $9 - (7 + 2) - 1 =$

45. $4 - (5 - 5) =$

46. $7 + (-7) - 1 =$

47. $10 + (-2) - 4 =$

48. $3 - (9 + 6) - 8 =$

49. $6 + (1 - 2) =$

50. $10 - 10 - 9 =$

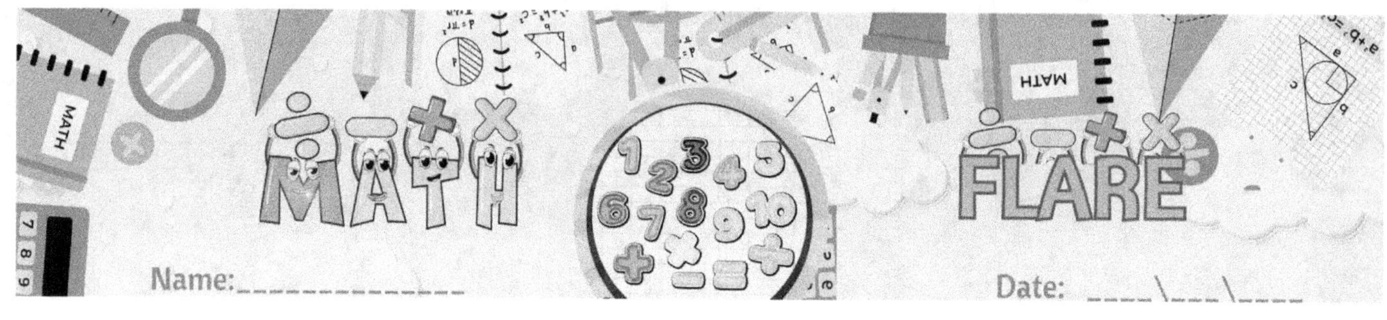

51. $5 - (1 + 7) + 3 =$

52. $2 - 2 - 9 =$

53. $3 + 8 - (2 + 10) =$

54. $8 + (-1) + 9 =$

55. $2 - (1 + 2) + 1 =$

56. $9 - (-8) - 3 =$

57. $4 - (2 - 5) =$

58. $5 - 3 + 4 =$

59. $(-2) + 5 + (-5) =$

60. $4 + 5 - 9 =$

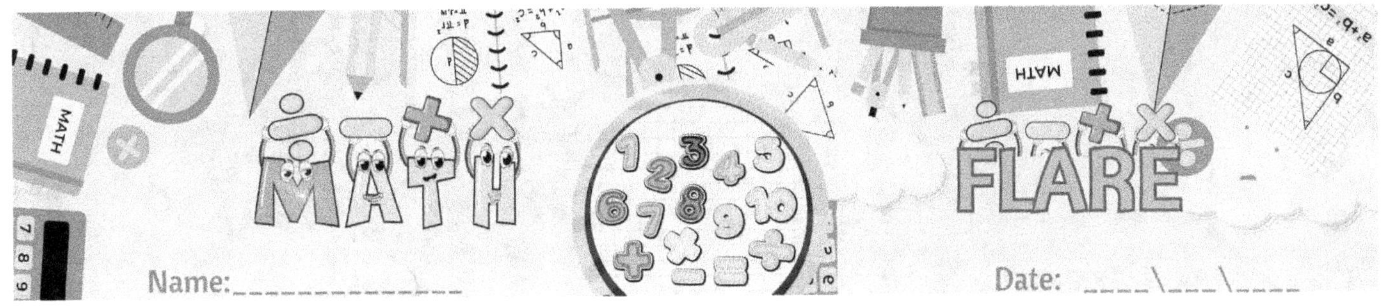

61. $8 - (8 + 10) - 7 =$

62. $2 - (-4) =$

63. $6 + (8 - 8) =$

64. $(-2) + (-1) + 5 =$

65. $5 - 8 + 8 =$

66. $6 + 6 - 10 + 1 =$

67. $1 + (-3) - 7 =$

68. $1 + 9 - (2 + 9) =$

69. $9 - 8 + 8 =$

70. $9 + 3 - (8 + 6) =$

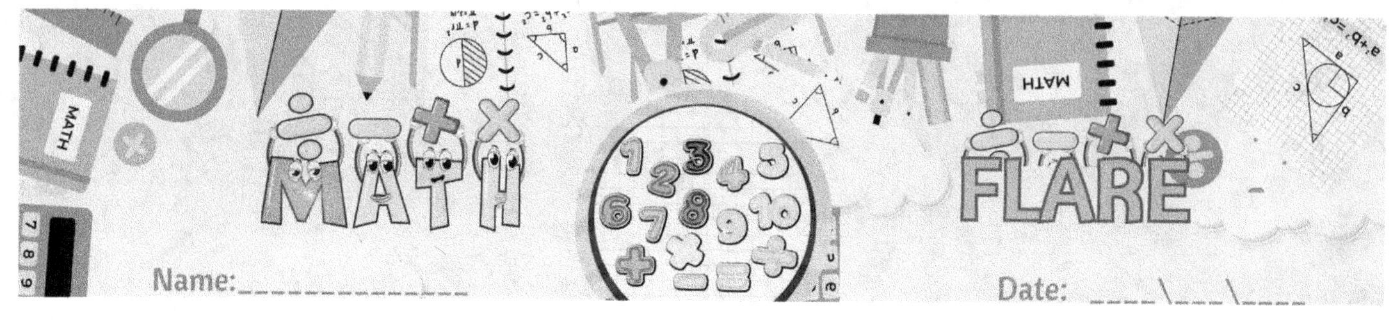

71. $9 + 4 - 1 =$

72. $2 + 4 - 1 =$

73. $8 - 3 - 1 - 5 =$

74. $3 - (2 + 1) - 10 =$

75. $5 + (-7) + 6 =$

76. $(-10) + 6 + (-4) =$

77. $4 + (7 - 2) =$

78. $8 + (-2) + 5 =$

79. $3 - (6 + 9) - 1 =$

80. $10 - (9 + 3) - 10 =$

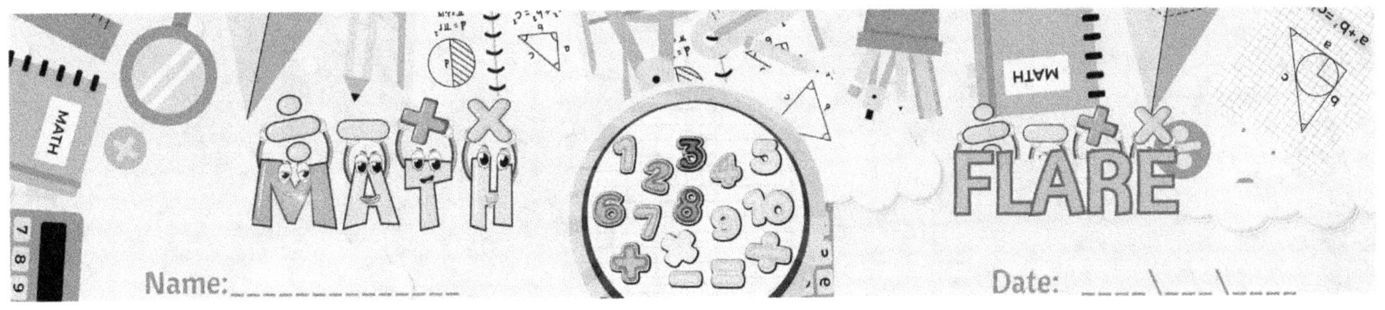

81. $7 + (5 - 7) =$

82. $4 - (-2) =$

83. $9 + 3 - (8 + 3) =$

84. $3 - 8 - (7 + 2) =$

85. $10 + (-4) =$

86. $1 - (2 + 10) - 8 =$

87. $(-5) + 3 + (-3) =$

88. $(-3) + 4 + (-1) =$

89. $9 - 9 - (3 + 5) =$

90. $10 - (-5) =$

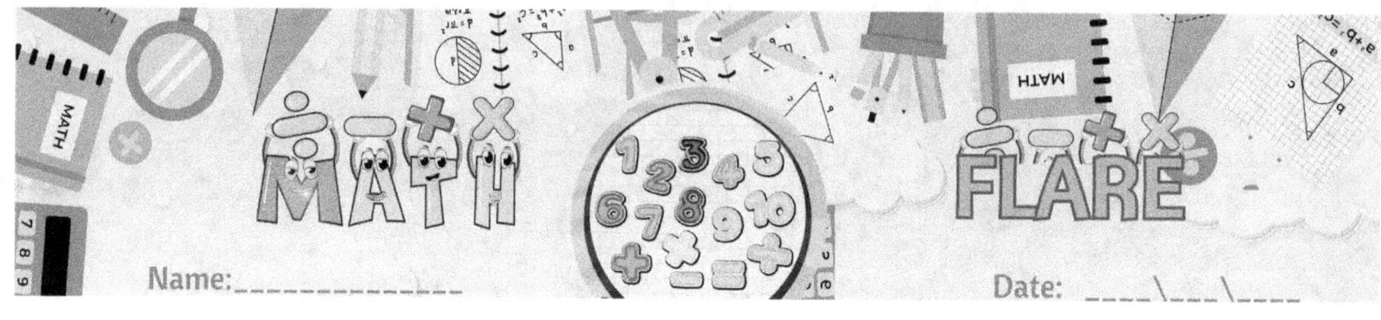

91. $5 - 10 - (2 + 3) =$

92. $1 - (1 + 3) + 8 =$

93. $7 - (1 + 6) + 4 =$

94. $9 - 10 - (6 + 4) =$

95. $3 + 2 - 8 =$

96. $9 + (-1) + 2 =$

97. $(-8) + (-8) + 4 =$

98. $3 - 3 - 4 - 3 =$

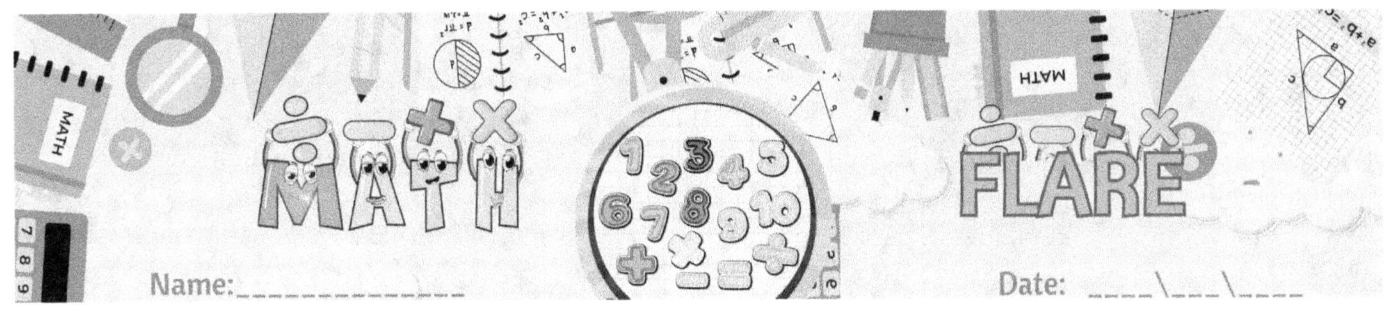

Operations with Decimals

Complete the operations.

1.
$$3.5 \times 4.1$$

2.
$$69.98 + 90.56$$

3.
$$91.01 - 70.43$$

4.
$$5.4 \overline{)9.0}$$

5.
$$1.3 \times 8.0$$

6.
$$50.70 - 20.12$$

7.
$$3.5 \overline{)8.3}$$

8.
$$89.00 + 38.00$$

9.
$$5.6 \times 7.9$$

10.
$$1.9 \times 3.4$$

11.
$$31.80 - 28.26$$

12.
$$66.11 - 20.43$$

13.

$3.6\overline{)2.2}$

14.

$$\begin{array}{r} 41.39 \\ +\ 21.78 \\ \hline \end{array}$$

15.

$$\begin{array}{r} 87.46 \\ -\ 15.55 \\ \hline \end{array}$$

16.

$5.0\overline{)3.3}$

17.

$5.4\overline{)7.1}$

18.

$8.7\overline{)5.5}$

19.

$$\begin{array}{r} 2.2 \\ \times\ 8.2 \\ \hline \end{array}$$

20.

$$\begin{array}{r} 51.92 \\ -\ 36.32 \\ \hline \end{array}$$

21.

$$\begin{array}{r} 1.1 \\ \times\ 8.5 \\ \hline \end{array}$$

22.

$$\begin{array}{r} 23.63 \\ +\ 53.65 \\ \hline \end{array}$$

23.

$$\begin{array}{r} 73.87 \\ -\ 18.44 \\ \hline \end{array}$$

24.

$$\begin{array}{r} 5.3 \\ \times\ 1.3 \\ \hline \end{array}$$

25.

$$\begin{array}{r} 88.18 \\ +\ 34.48 \\ \hline \end{array}$$

26.

$2.5\overline{)3.0}$

27.

$2.9\overline{)5.5}$

28.

$$\begin{array}{r} 89.89 \\ -\ 82.34 \\ \hline \end{array}$$

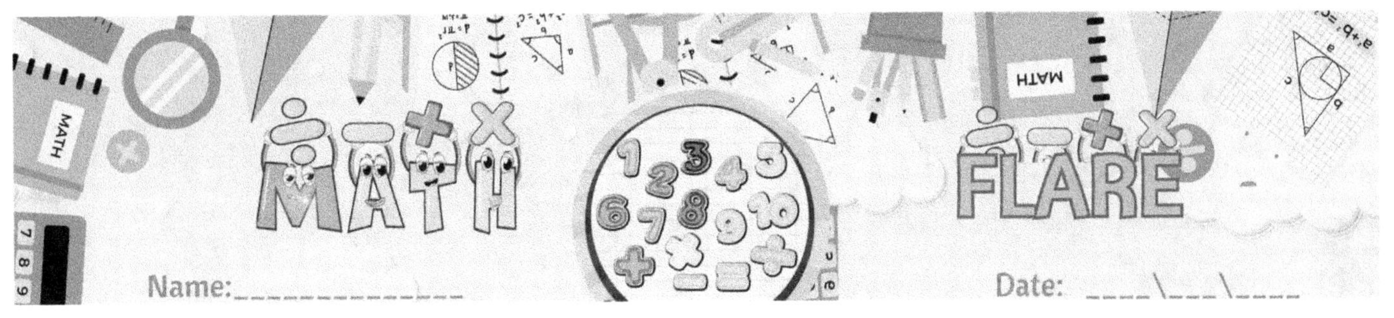

Name: _______________   Date: ____ \ ____ \ ____

29. 53.13 + 27.89	30. 56.30 + 45.39	31. 68.52 − 49.93	32. 83.77 + 44.59
33. 35.76 + 36.82	34. 3.7 × 1.7	35. 45.34 − 35.72	36. 9.8⟌6.0
37. 8.7 × 3.1	38. 1.7 × 5.8	39. 72.65 + 66.91	40. 38.85 + 89.27
41. 69.40 − 19.40	42. 77.07 + 22.60	43. 12.06 + 93.63	44. 1.7 × 6.3

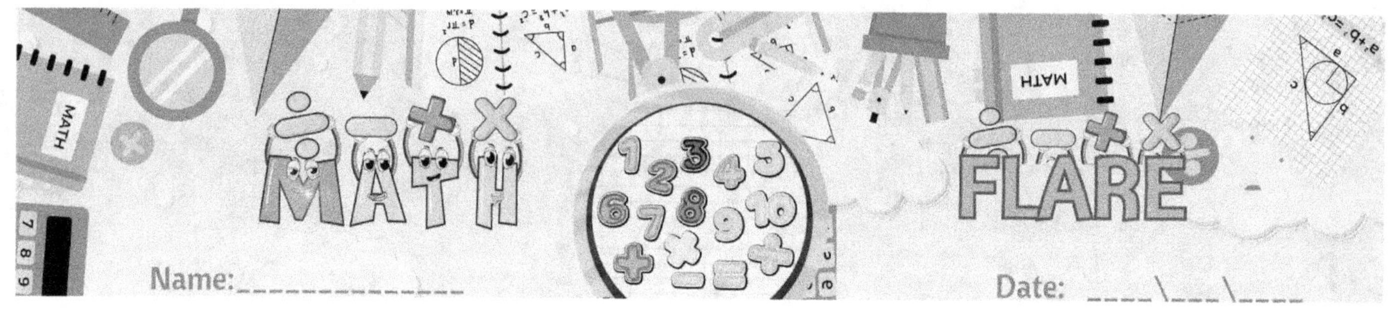

45. $8.3\overline{)9.2}$

46.
$$\begin{array}{r} 22.33 \\ +\ 72.30 \\ \hline \end{array}$$

47.
$$\begin{array}{r} 54.00 \\ -\ 35.35 \\ \hline \end{array}$$

48.
$$\begin{array}{r} 69.16 \\ -\ 36.08 \\ \hline \end{array}$$

49.
$$\begin{array}{r} 6.0 \\ \times\ 2.2 \\ \hline \end{array}$$

50.
$$\begin{array}{r} 60.78 \\ +\ 30.97 \\ \hline \end{array}$$

51.
$$\begin{array}{r} 68.65 \\ -\ 60.93 \\ \hline \end{array}$$

52.
$$\begin{array}{r} 89.34 \\ -\ 65.79 \\ \hline \end{array}$$

53.
$$\begin{array}{r} 58.18 \\ -\ 35.91 \\ \hline \end{array}$$

54.
$$\begin{array}{r} 7.3 \\ \times\ 8.4 \\ \hline \end{array}$$

55.
$$\begin{array}{r} 8.9 \\ \times\ 4.3 \\ \hline \end{array}$$

56.
$$\begin{array}{r} 6.4 \\ \times\ 6.6 \\ \hline \end{array}$$

57. $3.4\overline{)6.5}$

58. $4.8\overline{)4.0}$

59.
$$\begin{array}{r} 1.3 \\ \times\ 9.7 \\ \hline \end{array}$$

60.
$$\begin{array}{r} 9.5 \\ \times\ 3.9 \\ \hline \end{array}$$

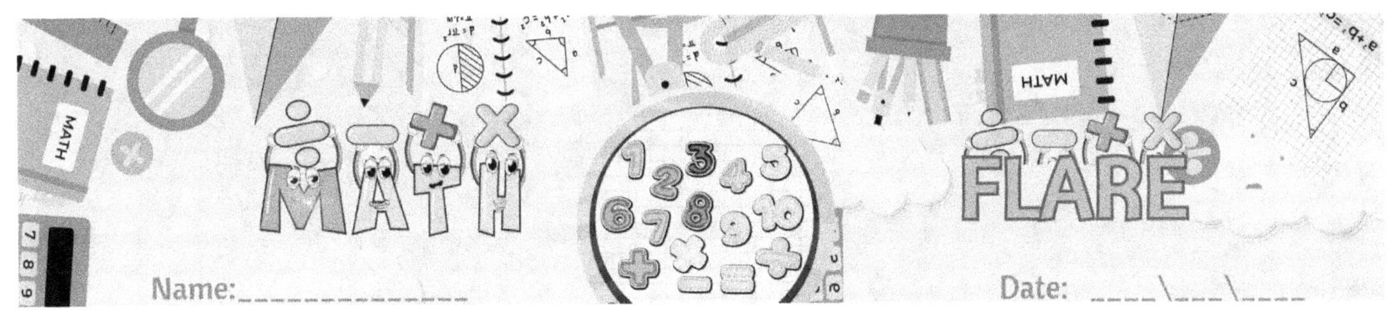

61.
$$4.7 \overline{)3.7}$$

62.
$$1.7 \overline{)7.2}$$

63.
$$\begin{array}{r} 15.44 \\ +\ 47.98 \\ \hline \end{array}$$

64.
$$\begin{array}{r} 43.03 \\ +\ 88.40 \\ \hline \end{array}$$

65.
$$\begin{array}{r} 6.8 \\ \times\ 4.5 \\ \hline \end{array}$$

66.
$$5.3 \overline{)1.4}$$

67.
$$\begin{array}{r} 67.96 \\ -\ 67.60 \\ \hline \end{array}$$

68.
$$\begin{array}{r} 3.4 \\ \times\ 2.1 \\ \hline \end{array}$$

69.
$$\begin{array}{r} 71.53 \\ +\ 49.39 \\ \hline \end{array}$$

70.
$$\begin{array}{r} 85.13 \\ -\ 83.75 \\ \hline \end{array}$$

71.
$$\begin{array}{r} 51.90 \\ -\ 26.94 \\ \hline \end{array}$$

72.
$$3.5 \overline{)6.2}$$

73.
$$\begin{array}{r} 72.08 \\ +\ 61.65 \\ \hline \end{array}$$

74.
$$\begin{array}{r} 94.94 \\ -\ 22.79 \\ \hline \end{array}$$

75.
$$3.0 \overline{)1.4}$$

76.
$$\begin{array}{r} 4.8 \\ \times\ 9.5 \\ \hline \end{array}$$

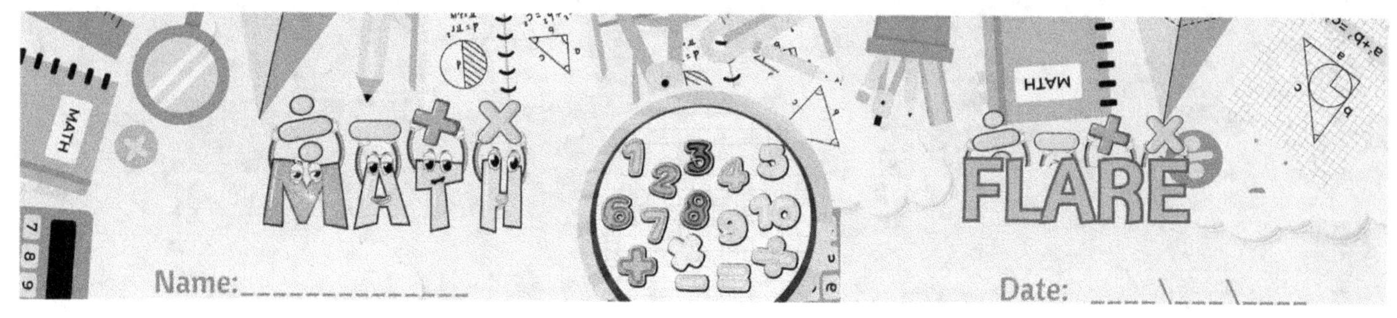

77. 99.27
   + 58.49

78. 7.1√1.1

79. 61.54
   - 27.56

80. 83.69
   - 48.78

81. 8.9
   × 1.7

82. 54.39
   + 38.41

83. 91.31
   - 41.85

84. 24.68
   - 18.58

85. 4.7
   × 6.8

86. 74.72
   - 55.05

87. 90.52
   - 70.24

88. 5.2
   × 8.0

89. 6.8
   × 2.9

90. 2.7
   × 9.4

91. 8.9√8.6

92. 98.77
   - 34.38

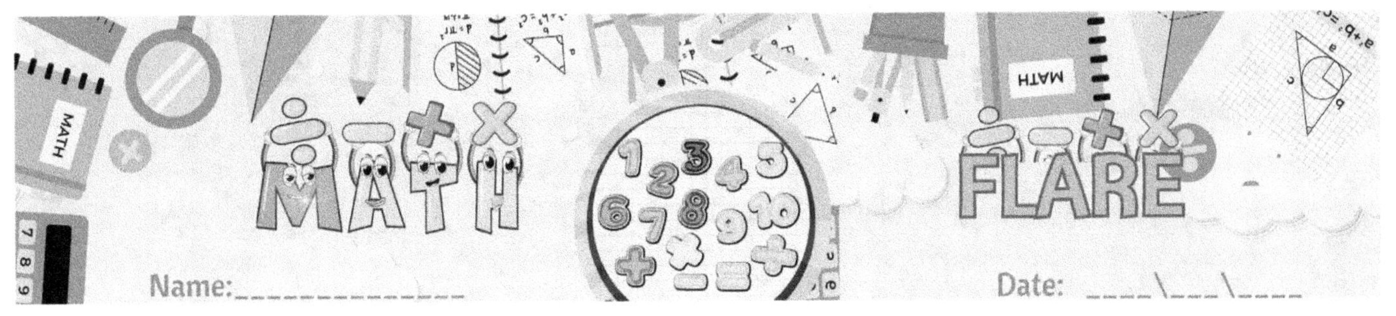

93.
84.35
+ 46.62

94.
3.6)5.7

95.
66.01
+ 92.38

96.
29.47
+ 88.57

97.
1.3
× 1.6

98.
9.6)7.3

99.
6.0
× 4.0

100.
66.53
+ 63.51

101.
5.4
× 7.1

102.
83.90
− 66.12

103.
44.54
+ 77.26

104.
8.0
× 8.9

105.
70.06
− 44.31

106.
34.28
+ 57.30

107.
68.77
− 54.78

108.
3.9)9.3

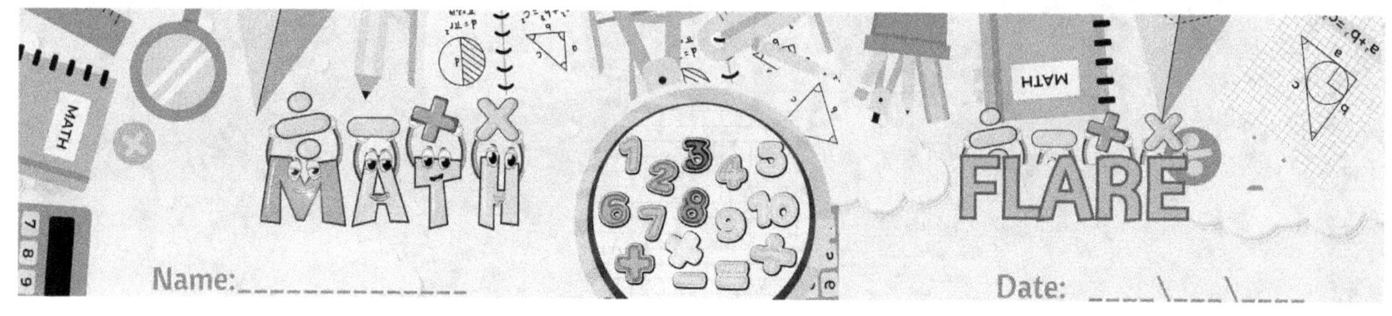

109. 1.8
× 7.1

110. 81.75
+ 80.70

111. 83.75
− 15.86

112. 44.12
− 21.40

113. 7.6 ⟌ 5.0

114. 8.9
× 7.5

115. 95.48
− 14.66

116. 6.9
× 5.6

117. 7.9
× 1.3

118. 8.7 ⟌ 2.4

119. 96.05
− 32.36

120. 8.6 ⟌ 3.1

121. 57.17
− 30.58

122. 8.9
× 2.4

123. 24.48
+ 77.39

124. 36.93
+ 47.76

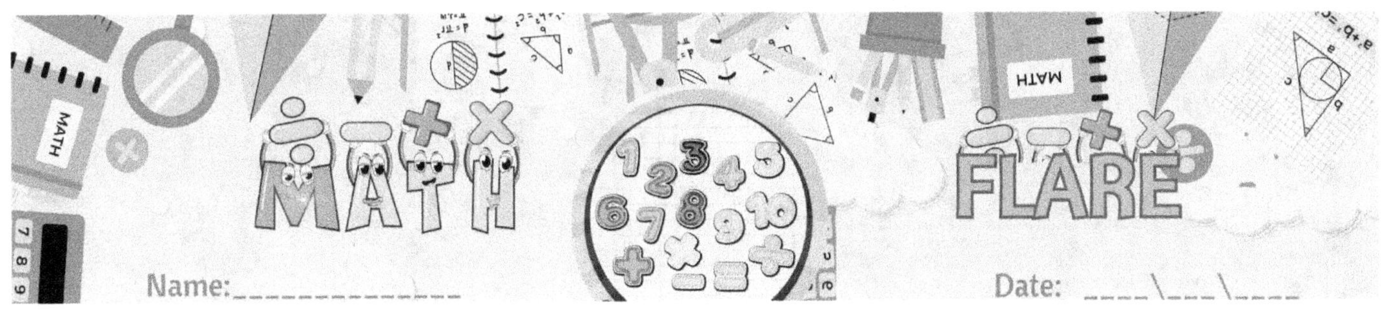

125.
$$99.44 + 51.31$$

126.
$$4.8 \overline{)6.4}$$

127.
$$1.5 \overline{)9.8}$$

128.
$$6.6 \overline{)8.3}$$

129.
$$4.4 \overline{)2.4}$$

130.
$$60.39 - 45.80$$

131.
$$4.5 \times 9.1$$

132.
$$7.4 \overline{)9.8}$$

133.
$$8.1 \times 7.6$$

134.
$$8.2 \times 2.0$$

135.
$$92.87 + 68.20$$

136.
$$30.03 + 16.14$$

137.
$$6.8 \times 1.0$$

138.
$$2.6 \overline{)6.3}$$

139.
$$84.85 + 67.89$$

140.
$$71.14 - 54.14$$

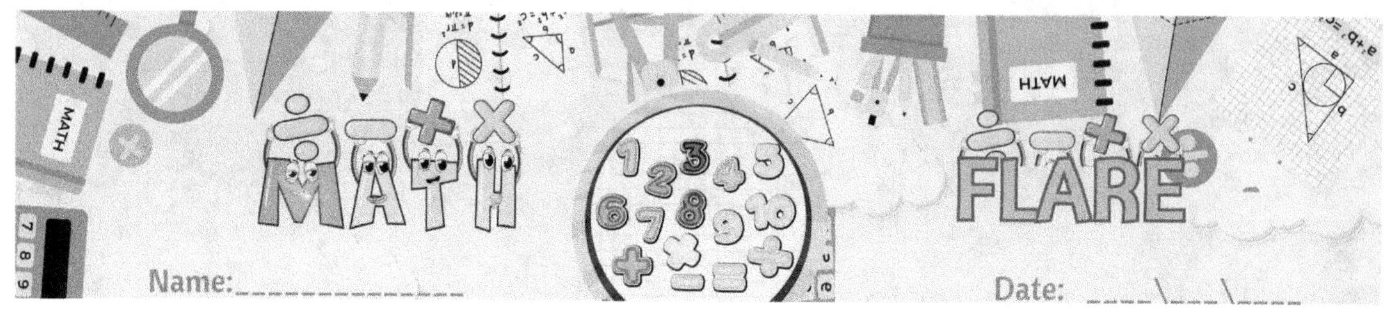

141. 73.85
    + 45.38

142. 50.44
    − 47.24

143. 72.49
    + 74.11

144. 90.71
    − 70.10

145. 2.8$\overline{)4.5}$

146. 3.0$\overline{)9.1}$

147.   2.6
    × 9.1

148. 9.9$\overline{)8.3}$

149. 37.54
    + 25.15

150. 71.30
    − 45.02

151. 97.48
    − 15.60

152. 8.2$\overline{)2.4}$

153. 7.0$\overline{)4.1}$

154. 23.51
    + 11.43

155. 15.92
    + 41.44

156. 6.5$\overline{)5.1}$

157. 58.21
    − 48.69

158. 56.58
    + 19.67

159.   6.9
     × 9.1

160.   2.6
     × 7.0

161. 6.9)2.0

162. 1.1)4.0

163. 5.9)9.7

164.   2.5
     × 7.0

165.   6.3
     × 9.6

166.   4.7
     × 6.5

167. 24.72
    − 13.06

168.   8.3
     × 9.5

169. 75.15
    + 33.75

170.   6.5
     × 4.4

171. 66.16
    − 41.00

172. 8.4)3.3

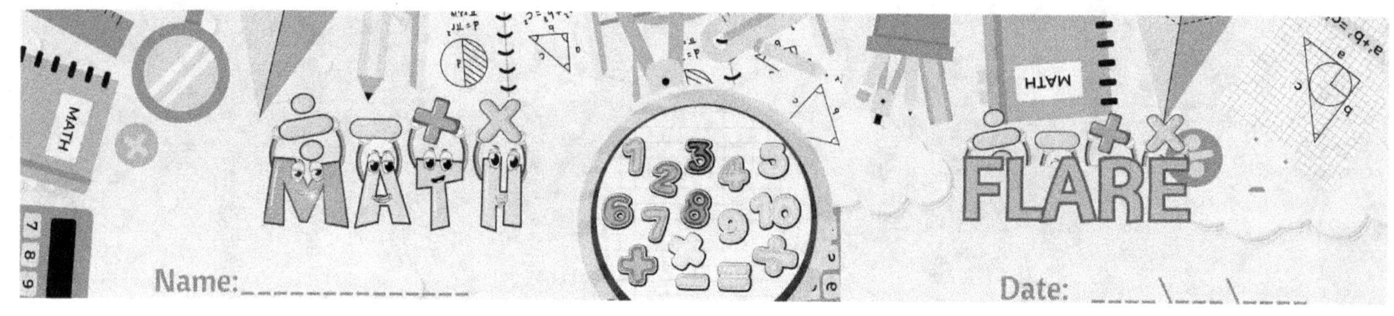

Name:________________ Date: _______________

173. 16.76
    + 97.26

174. 2.7)8.5

175. 86.42
    + 38.18

176. 24.68
    + 85.72

177. 17.64
    + 90.82

178. 2.4)8.8

179. 35.90
    + 94.68

180. 9.8)3.6

181. 4.5)4.6

182. 97.60
    - 22.92

183. 5.2)5.7

184. 35.70
    + 62.50

185. 1.3
    × 7.6

186. 59.04
    + 14.07

187. 45.54
    + 27.13

188. 1.6
    × 2.5

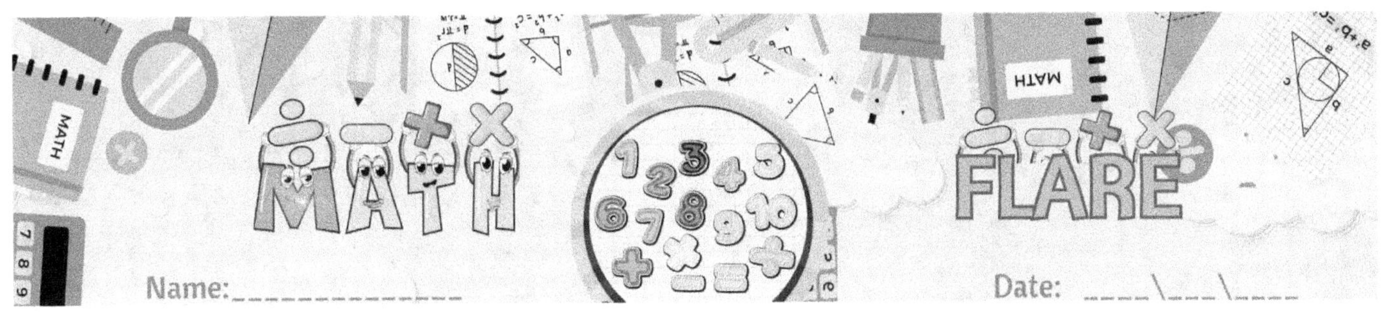

189. 8.2)‾9.0‾

190. 4.7
    × 9.1

191. 5.7)‾7.2‾

192. 88.40
    − 66.79

193. 57.73
    − 40.60

194. 7.5)‾6.1‾

195. 3.0)‾4.7‾

196. 8.7
    × 4.9

197. 77.29
    − 37.79

198. 67.45
    − 23.14

199. 89.02
    − 62.46

200. 27.58
    + 60.86

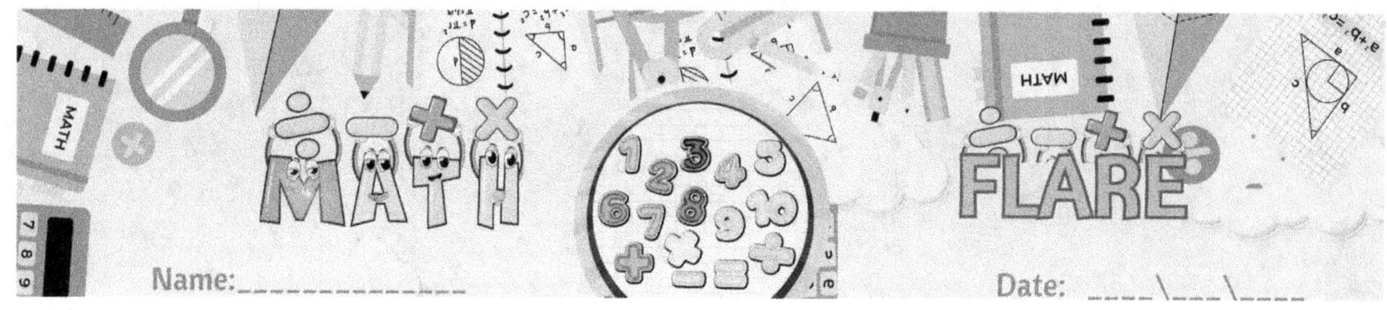

Exponents

Convert the values.

1. $15^2 =$ _______________

2. $9^4 =$ _______________

3. $11^2 =$ _______________

4. $4^2 =$ _______________

5. $10^3 =$ _______________

6. $17^2 =$ _______________

7. $11^{-3} =$ _______________

8. $14^3 =$ _______________

9. $11^{-2} =$ _______________

10. $18^4 =$ _______________

11. $18^2 =$ _______________

12. $5^{-3} =$ _______________

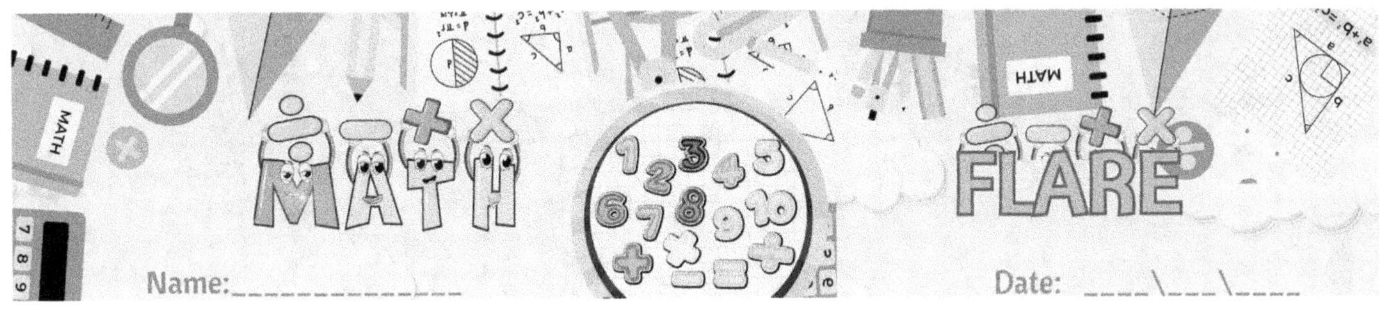

13. $16^{-2} =$

14. $1^2 =$

15. $17^4 =$

16. $8^{-2} =$

17. $2^3 =$

18. $3^{-2} =$

19. $11^3 =$

20. $13^{-3} =$

21. $2^{-2} =$

22. $4^{-2} =$

23. $9^{-3} =$

24. $8^2 =$

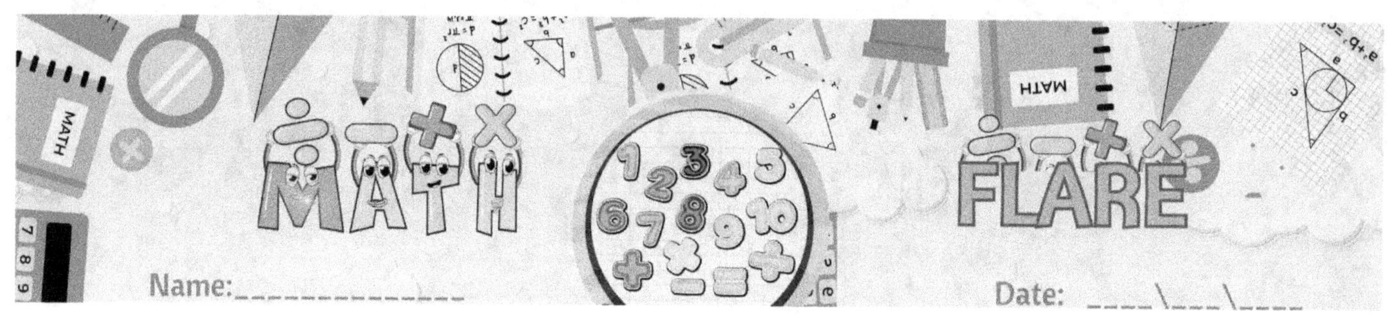

25. 20^{-3} = _________________

26. 19^{3} = _________________

27. 9^{2} = _________________

28. 15^{-3} = _________________

29. 12^{-2} = _________________

30. 12^{-3} = _________________

31. 7^{2} = _________________

32. 6^{-3} = _________________

33. 15^{4} = _________________

34. 2^{-3} = _________________

35. 13^{2} = _________________

36. 19^{4} = _________________

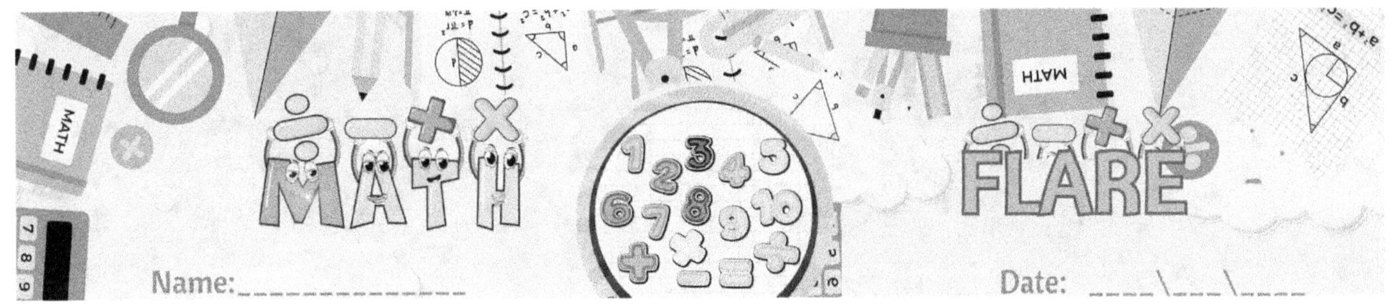

Name:______________________   Date: _____________

37. $16^3 =$ _______________

38. $10^{-2} =$ _______________

39. $16^4 =$ _______________

40. $3^3 =$ _______________

41. $1^3 =$ _______________

42. $20^2 =$ _______________

43. $9^{-2} =$ _______________

44. $7^3 =$ _______________

45. $12^4 =$ _______________

46. $1^4 =$ _______________

47. $4^{-3} =$ _______________

48. $5^3 =$ _______________

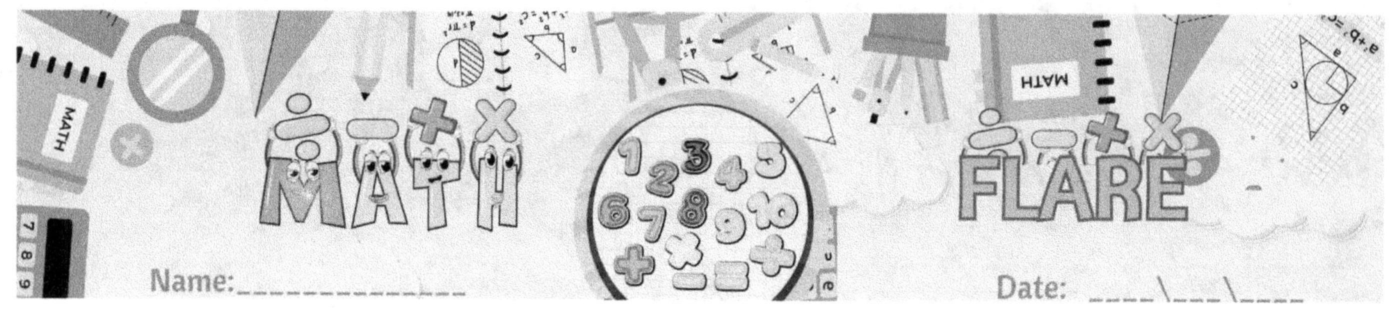

49. 8^{-3} =

50. 17^{-3} =

51. 2^{4} =

52. 15^{-2} =

53. 19^{-3} =

54. 5^{2} =

55. 1^{-3} =

56. 20^{3} =

57. 4^{3} =

58. 16^{2} =

59. 14^{-2} =

60. 12^{3} =

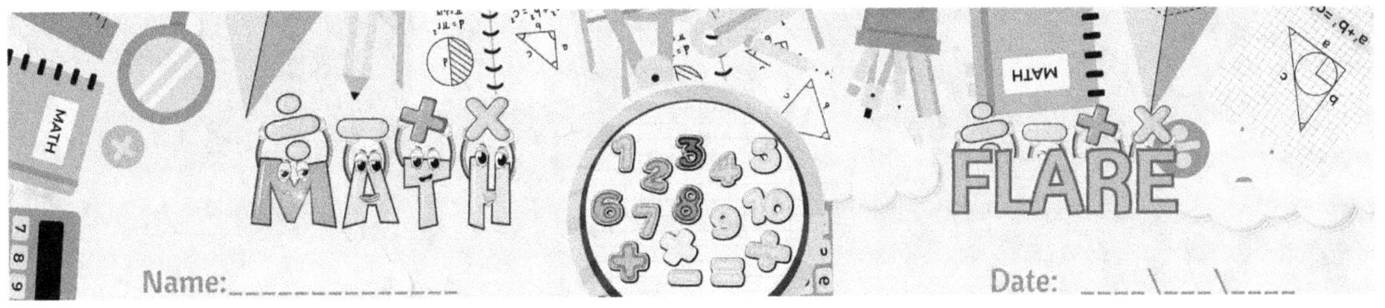

Square and Cube Roots

Calculate the root of each value.

1. $\sqrt[3]{343}$ = ______________________

2. $\sqrt{4}$ = ______________________

3. $\sqrt[4]{1{,}296}$ = ______________________

4. $\sqrt[4]{1}$ = ______________________

5. $\sqrt[4]{16}$ = ______________________

6. $\sqrt[4]{2{,}401}$ = ______________________

7. $\sqrt[4]{6{,}561}$ = ______________________

8. $\sqrt{7{,}225}$ = ______________________

9. $\sqrt[3]{1{,}728}$ = ______________________

10. $\sqrt{676}$ = ______________________

11. $\sqrt[3]{5{,}832}$ = ______________________

12. $\sqrt[3]{216}$ = ______________________

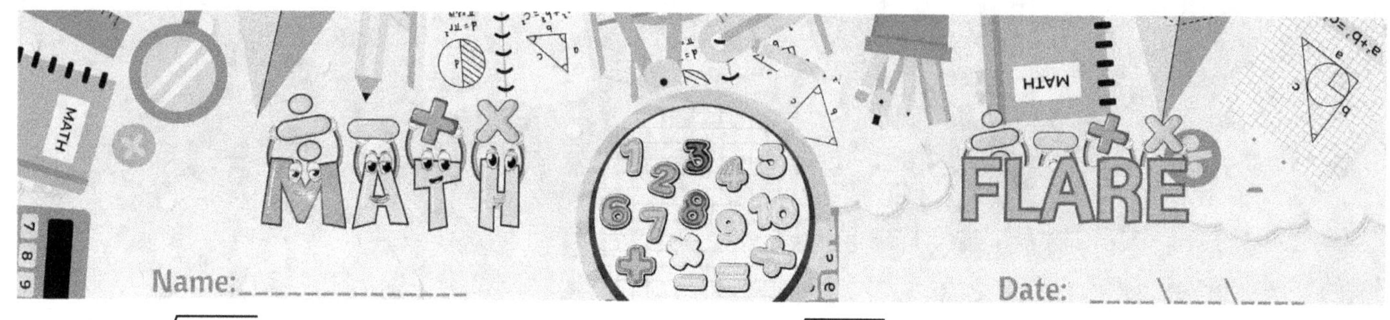

13. $\sqrt{484}$ = _______________

14. $\sqrt[4]{256}$ = _______________

15. $\sqrt[3]{1{,}000}$ = _______________

16. $\sqrt{1}$ = _______________

17. $\sqrt[3]{8}$ = _______________

18. $\sqrt[4]{81}$ = _______________

19. $\sqrt[3]{125}$ = _______________

20. $\sqrt{36}$ = _______________

21. $\sqrt{225}$ = _______________

22. $\sqrt{16}$ = _______________

23. $\sqrt[3]{3{,}375}$ = _______________

24. $\sqrt{100}$ = _______________

25. $\sqrt{25}$ = _______________

26. $\sqrt[4]{4{,}096}$ = _______________

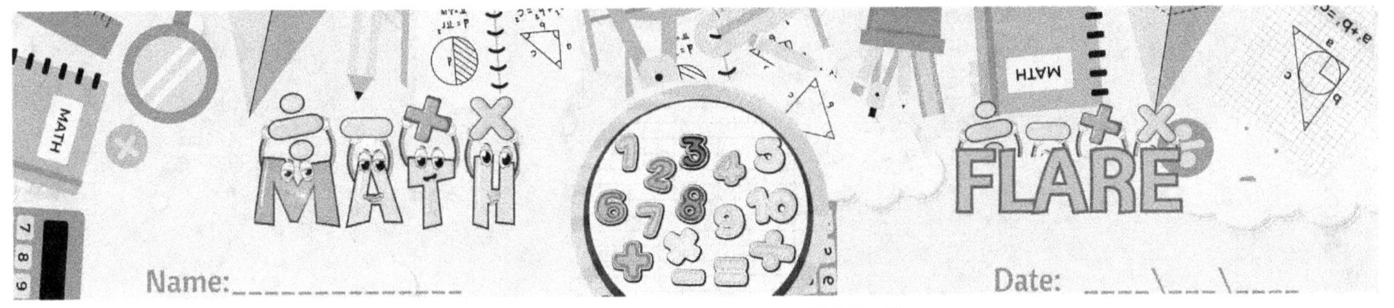

27. $\sqrt{49}$ = _________________

28. $\sqrt{2,116}$ = _________________

29. $\sqrt{64}$ = _________________

30. $\sqrt[3]{1}$ = _________________

31. $\sqrt{784}$ = _________________

32. $\sqrt{576}$ = _________________

33. $\sqrt{3,721}$ = _________________

34. $\sqrt[3]{64}$ = _________________

35. $\sqrt{1,849}$ = _________________

36. $\sqrt[3]{1,331}$ = _________________

37. $\sqrt{3,481}$ = _________________

38. $\sqrt{9}$ = _________________

39. $\sqrt{361}$ = _________________

40. $\sqrt{2,809}$ = _________________

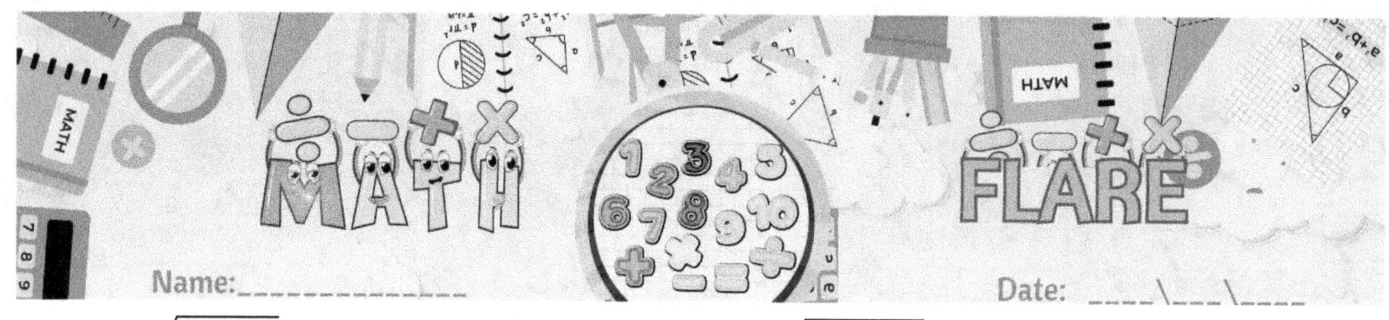

41. $\sqrt{2{,}916}$ = _______________

42. $\sqrt{6{,}400}$ = _______________

43. $\sqrt[3]{729}$ = _______________

44. $\sqrt[3]{27}$ = _______________

45. $\sqrt{81}$ = _______________

46. $\sqrt{2{,}601}$ = _______________

47. $\sqrt{3{,}249}$ = _______________

48. $\sqrt[3]{4{,}913}$ = _______________

49. $\sqrt{5{,}776}$ = _______________

50. $\sqrt[4]{10{,}000}$ = _______________

51. $\sqrt{3{,}364}$ = _______________

52. $\sqrt[3]{512}$ = _______________

53. $\sqrt{1{,}369}$ = _______________

54. $\sqrt{1{,}600}$ = _______________

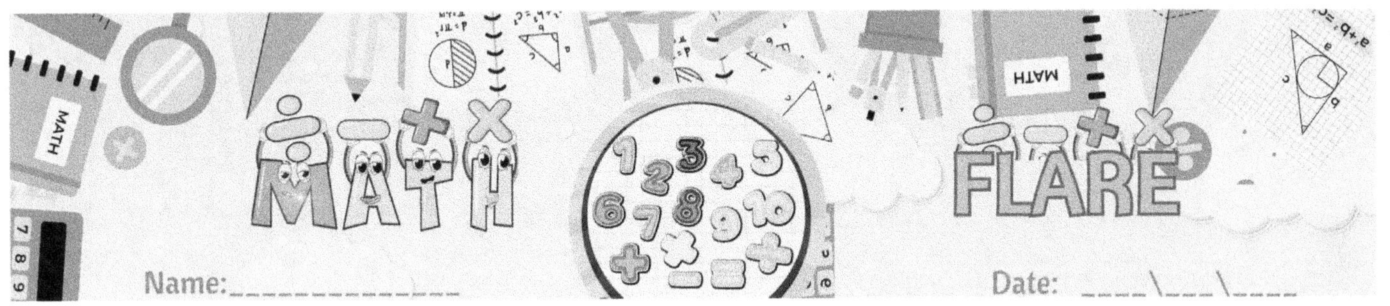

55. $\sqrt[3]{6{,}859}$ = ______________

56. $\sqrt{5{,}041}$ = ______________

57. $\sqrt{196}$ = ______________

58. $\sqrt{841}$ = ______________

59. $\sqrt{3{,}969}$ = ______________

60. $\sqrt{1{,}444}$ = ______________

61. $\sqrt{1{,}764}$ = ______________

62. $\sqrt[3]{10{,}648}$ = ______________

63. $\sqrt{961}$ = ______________

64. $\sqrt{289}$ = ______________

65. $\sqrt{5{,}929}$ = ______________

66. $\sqrt{6{,}241}$ = ______________

67. $\sqrt[4]{625}$ = ______________

68. $\sqrt{2{,}209}$ = ______________

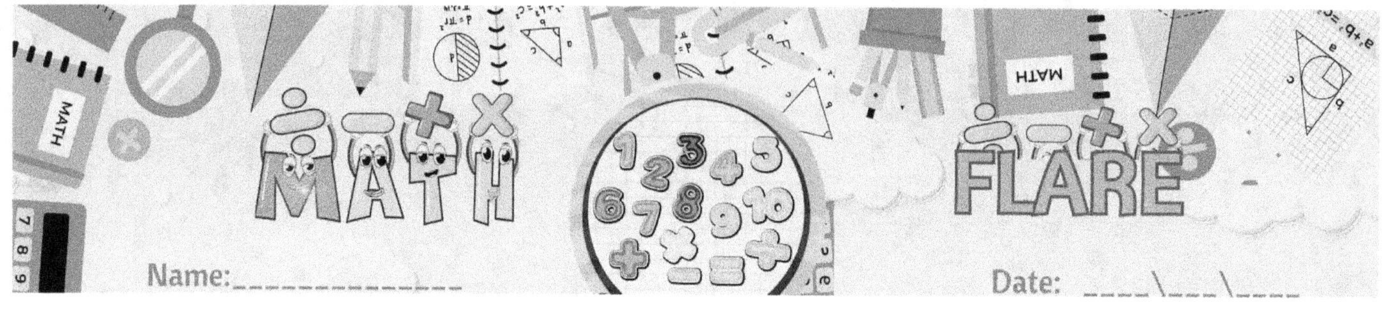

Multiple Operations with Fractions

Find the solution.

1. $\dfrac{3}{8} + \dfrac{7}{8} + \dfrac{1}{8} =$

2. $\dfrac{2}{3} + \dfrac{1}{2} + \dfrac{3}{8} =$

3. $\dfrac{1}{5} + \dfrac{3}{4} + \dfrac{3}{4} + \dfrac{7}{10} =$

4. $\dfrac{1}{5} + \dfrac{1}{6} + \dfrac{1}{2} =$

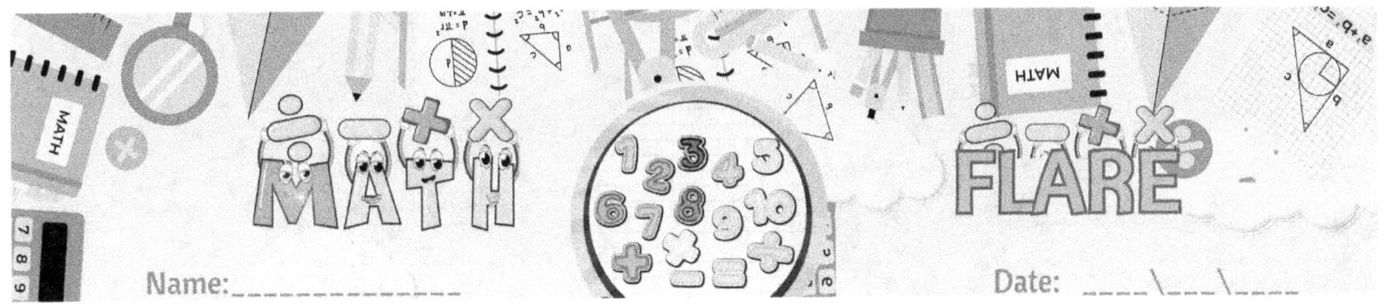

5. $\dfrac{2}{3} + \dfrac{3}{8} - \dfrac{3}{10} =$

6. $\dfrac{1}{4} + \dfrac{1}{8} + \dfrac{2}{5} + \dfrac{1}{6} =$

7. $\dfrac{3}{10} + \dfrac{7}{8} - \dfrac{3}{8} =$

8. $\dfrac{1}{2} + \dfrac{7}{8} + \dfrac{7}{8} =$

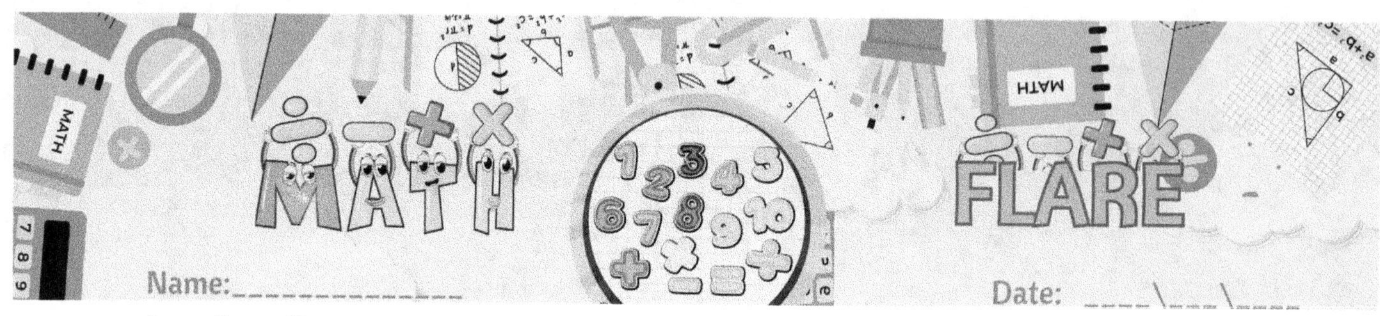

9. $\dfrac{1}{2} + \dfrac{5}{7} - \dfrac{3}{7} =$

10. $\dfrac{3}{8} + \dfrac{3}{4} + \dfrac{1}{4} + \dfrac{5}{8} =$

11. $\dfrac{2}{7} + \dfrac{1}{6} + \dfrac{3}{4} =$

12. $\dfrac{3}{10} \times \dfrac{3}{10} \times \dfrac{7}{10} =$

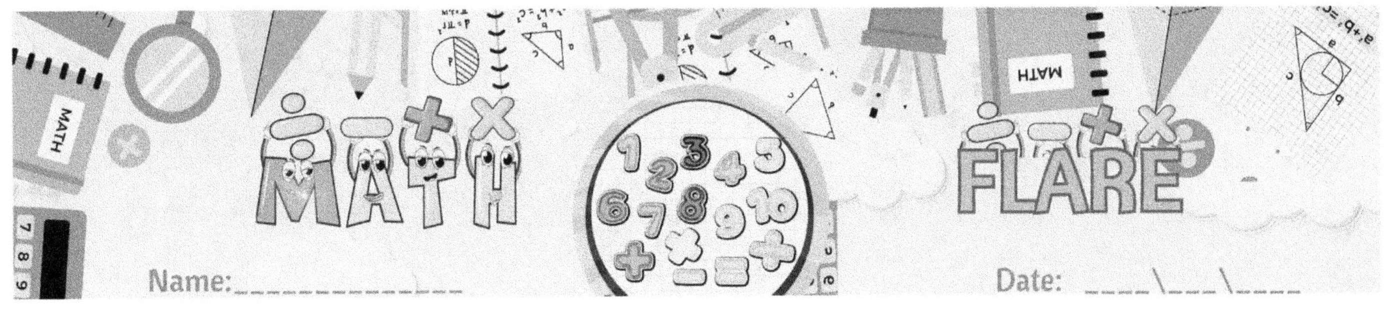

13. $\dfrac{1}{4} + \dfrac{1}{3} + \dfrac{2}{7} =$

14. $\dfrac{1}{6} + \dfrac{1}{5} + \dfrac{3}{4} =$

15. $\dfrac{3}{4} + \dfrac{1}{4} + \dfrac{5}{8} + \dfrac{2}{3} =$

16. $\dfrac{2}{3} + \dfrac{3}{8} - \dfrac{1}{6} =$

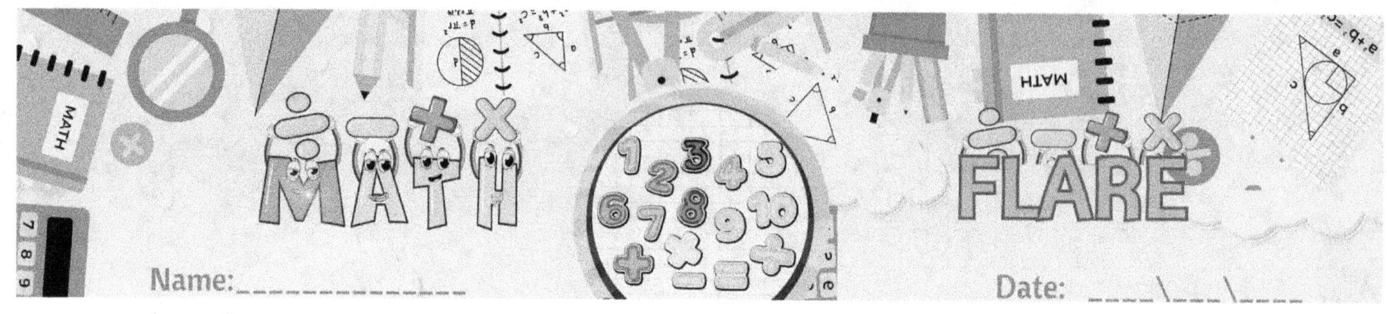

17. $\dfrac{1}{6} \times \dfrac{1}{5} \times \dfrac{7}{10} =$

18. $\dfrac{1}{4} + \dfrac{1}{2} + \dfrac{5}{8} + \dfrac{5}{6} =$

19. $\dfrac{4}{7} + \dfrac{5}{8} + \dfrac{4}{9} + \dfrac{2}{3} =$

20. $\dfrac{3}{7} + \dfrac{1}{2} - \dfrac{4}{7} =$

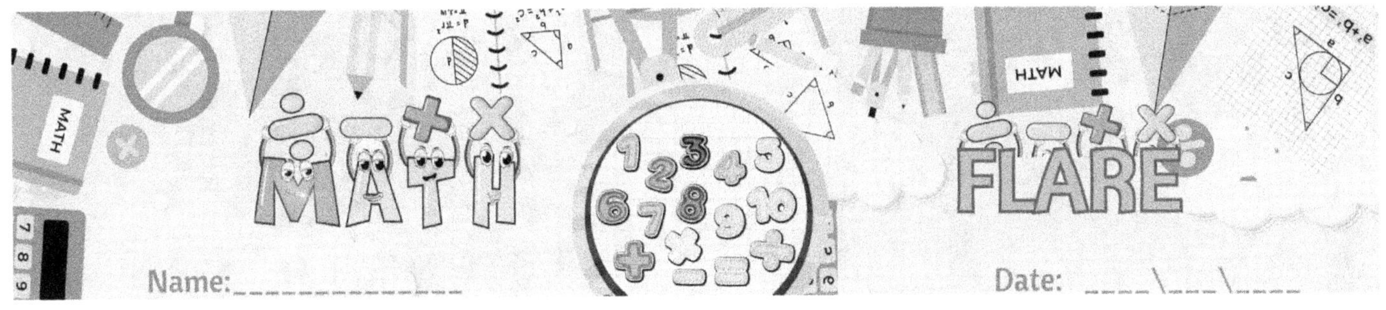

21. $\dfrac{5}{7} + \dfrac{7}{9} - \dfrac{1}{3} =$

22. $\dfrac{2}{3} + \dfrac{2}{3} - \dfrac{1}{4} =$

23. $\dfrac{4}{7} + \dfrac{1}{6} + \dfrac{1}{2} =$

24. $\dfrac{3}{7} + \dfrac{3}{10} - \dfrac{1}{8} =$

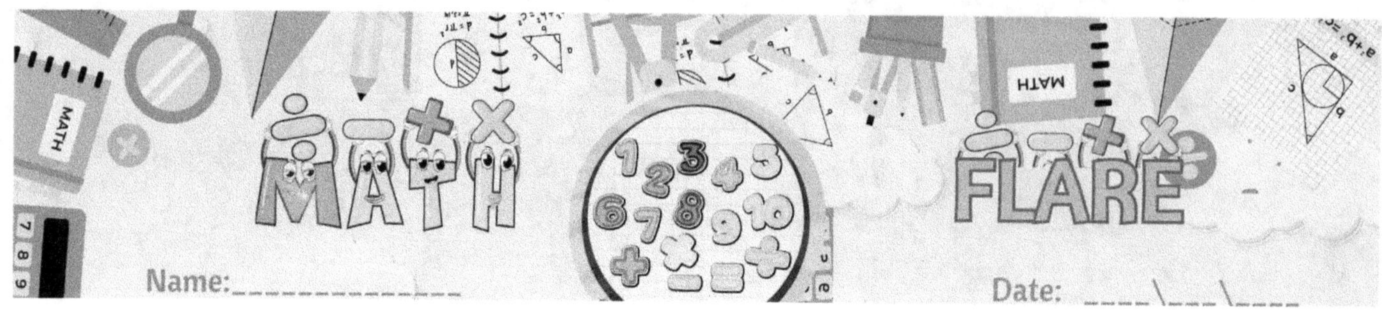

25. $\dfrac{3}{5} + \dfrac{1}{10} + \dfrac{1}{2} =$

26. $\dfrac{7}{8} + \dfrac{1}{5} + \dfrac{4}{9} + \dfrac{1}{9} =$

27. $\dfrac{1}{8} + \dfrac{7}{9} + \dfrac{1}{4} + \dfrac{1}{6} =$

28. $\dfrac{3}{4} + \dfrac{3}{7} + \dfrac{2}{3} =$

29. $\dfrac{1}{3} + \dfrac{1}{8} + \dfrac{3}{7} + \dfrac{2}{3} =$

30. $\dfrac{1}{6} \times \dfrac{1}{8} \times \dfrac{3}{10} =$

31. $\dfrac{1}{2} \times \dfrac{1}{2} \times \dfrac{1}{2} =$

32. $\dfrac{1}{2} \times \dfrac{1}{3} \times \dfrac{1}{2} =$

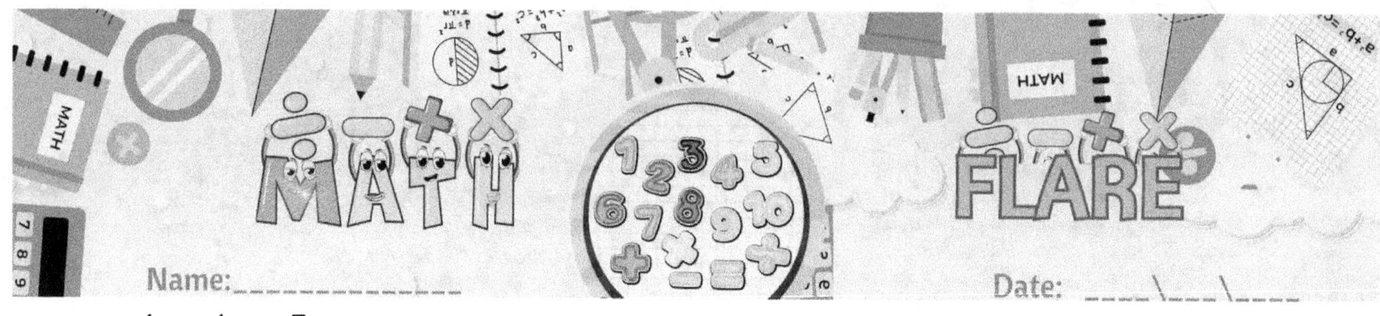

33. $\dfrac{1}{7} \times \dfrac{1}{6} \times \dfrac{3}{10} =$

34. $\dfrac{1}{2} + \dfrac{2}{7} + \dfrac{2}{9} + \dfrac{4}{9} =$

35. $\dfrac{1}{6} + \dfrac{7}{8} - \dfrac{8}{9} =$

36. $\dfrac{4}{5} \times \dfrac{1}{4} \times \dfrac{2}{9} =$

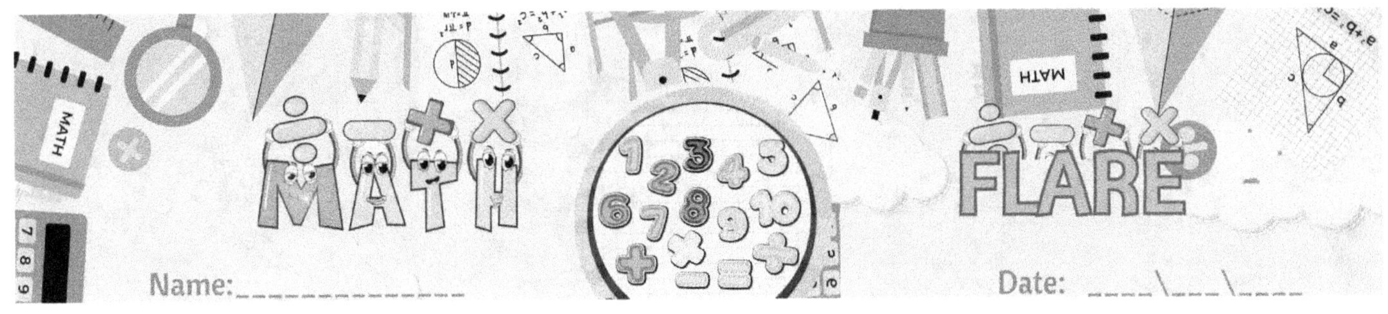

37. $\dfrac{3}{10} + \dfrac{1}{2} + \dfrac{3}{4} =$

38. $\dfrac{1}{9} + \dfrac{1}{4} + \dfrac{5}{9} =$

39. $\dfrac{1}{7} + \dfrac{1}{9} + \dfrac{5}{6} =$

40. $\dfrac{1}{2} + \dfrac{5}{8} - \dfrac{4}{9} =$

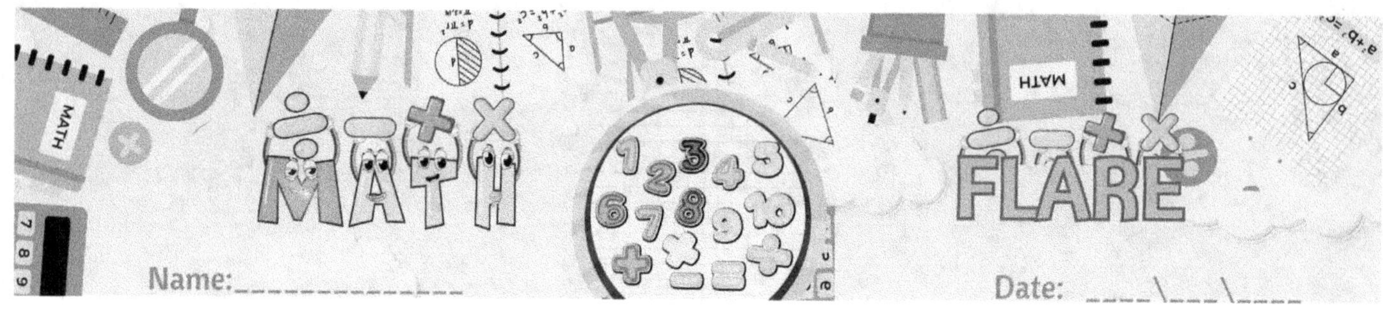

Convert: Ratio, Fraction, Percent, and Decimals

1.

	Ratio	Fraction	Percent	Decimal
a.			29.4%	
b.			90.9%	
c.			93.3%	
d.				0.111
e.				0.125
f.		8/9		
g.			77.8%	
h.				0.5
i.				1
j.		1/3		
k.				0.5
l.				0.769
m.			30%	
n.	4:9			
o.		8/10		

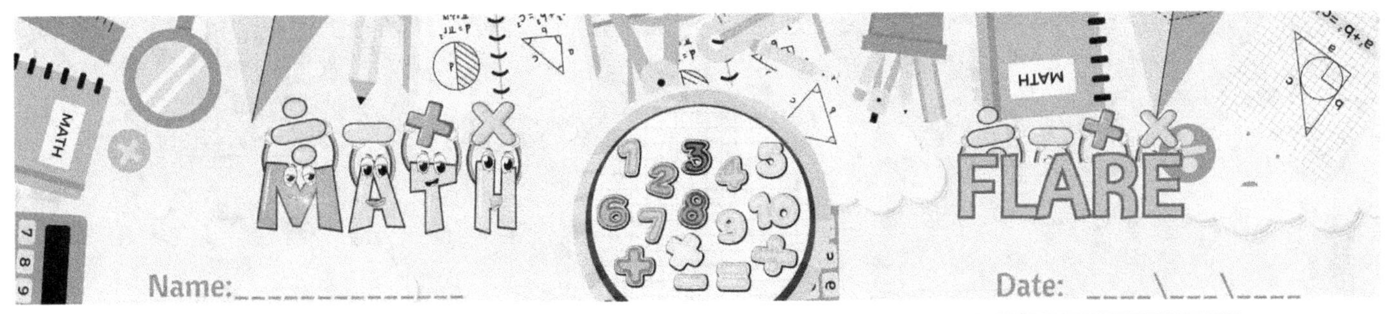

2.

	Ratio	Fraction	Percent	Decimal
a.	4:4			
b.			33.3%	
c.			26.3%	
d.	3:13			
e.		7/17		
f.				0.222
g.			12.5%	
h.				0.474
i.	5:12			
j.	11:13			
k.		4/9		
l.			21.1%	
m.	9:12			
n.		2/14		
o.			88.9%	

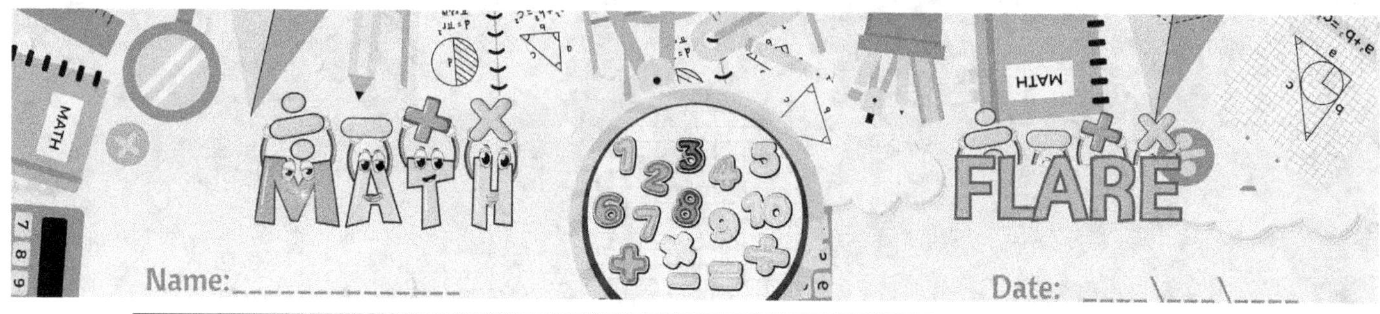

3.

	Ratio	Fraction	Percent	Decimal
a.	15:16			
b.				0.857
c.	4:14			
d.	3:5			
e.				0.889
f.				0.333
g.				0.1
h.		5/15		
i.		2/5		
j.	8:15			
k.			57.1%	
l.				0.833
m.				0.882
n.	5:6			
o.				0.667

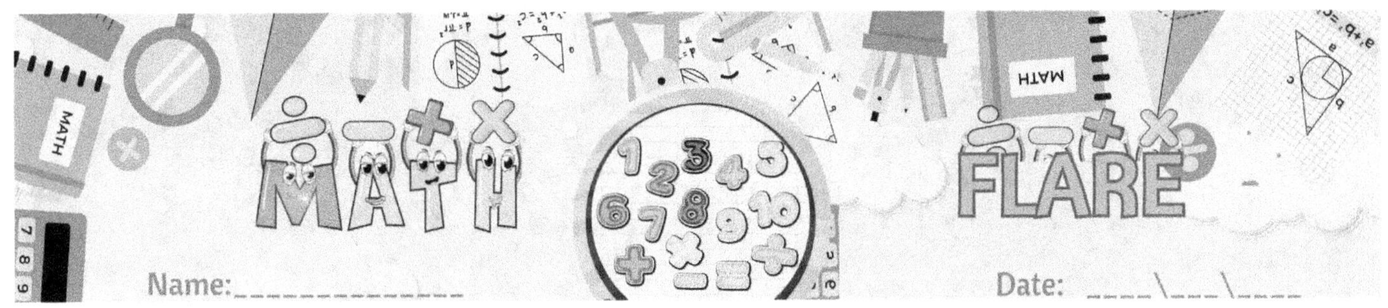

4.

	Ratio	Fraction	Percent	Decimal
a.		2/14		
b.	3:4			
c.		5/14		
d.				1
e.	2:6			
f.				0.6
g.			42.1%	
h.	13:19			
i.		4/15		
j.	1:3			
k.			30.8%	
l.	4:10			
m.			80%	
n.		7/14		
o.		6/14		

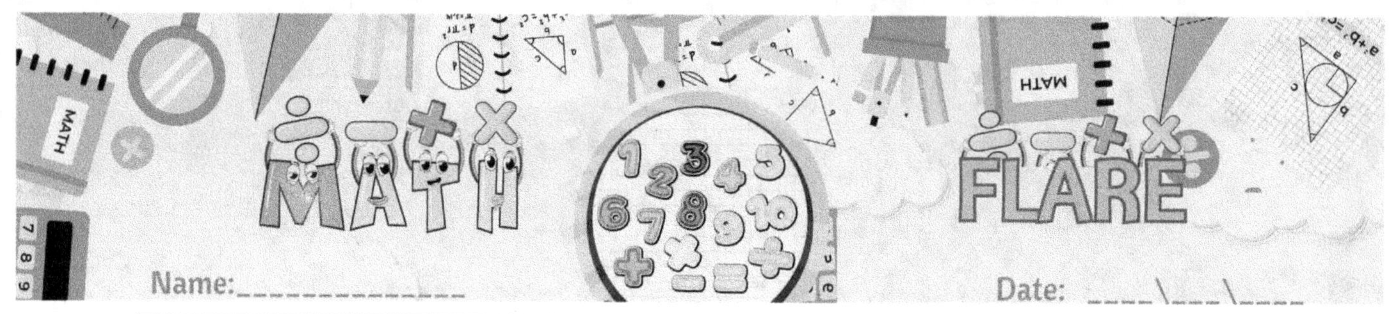

5.

	Ratio	Fraction	Percent	Decimal
a.				0.714
b.			66.7%	
c.		5/14		
d.			84.6%	
e.	3:10			
f.			33.3%	
g.				0.286
h.			89.5%	
i.		9/18		
j.			50%	
k.		9/20		
l.		10/10		
m.		9/10		
n.			22.2%	
o.		6/14		

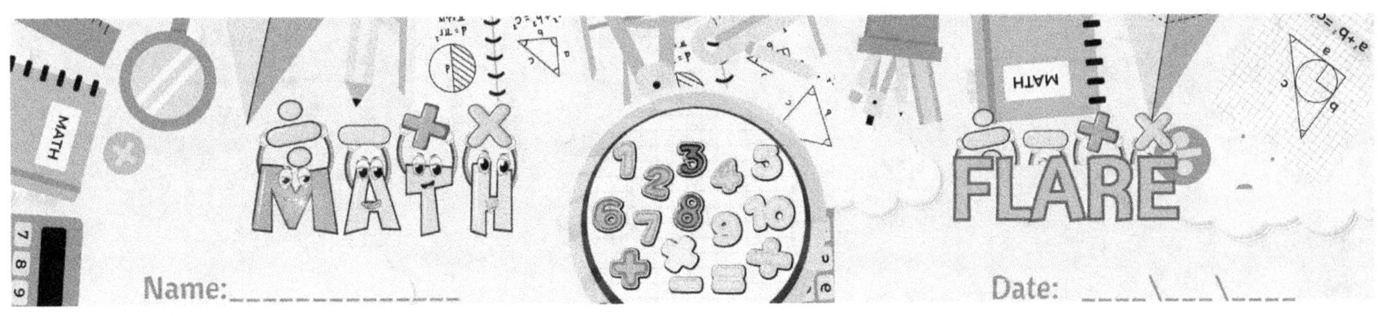

Solving One-Step Equations

Solve for the variable.

1. $\dfrac{m}{1} = 4$

2. $-7b = -35$

3. $5y = 20$

4. $-3a = -9$

5. $z + 4 = 14$

6. $49 = 7a$

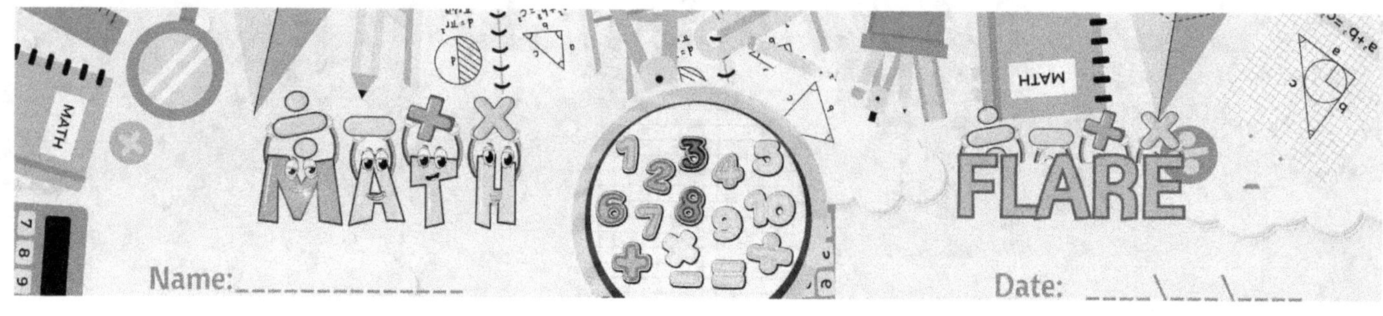

7. $-3 = -6 + a$

8. $-2 = -2m$

9. $k - 6 = 0$

10. $-x = -5$

11. $-6 = -2x$

12. $\dfrac{k}{1} = 6$

13. $-7m = -56$

14. $1 = \dfrac{a}{6}$

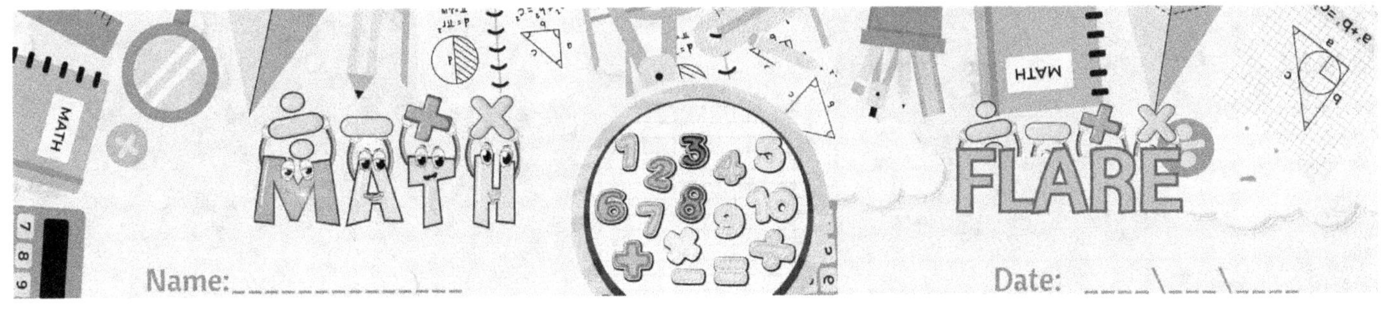

15. $y - 6 = -4$

16. $-2 + s = 1$

17. $21 = 3a$

18. $\dfrac{a}{4} = 1$

19. $9y = 9$

20. $2k = 6$

21. $3y = 30$

22. $-10b = -50$

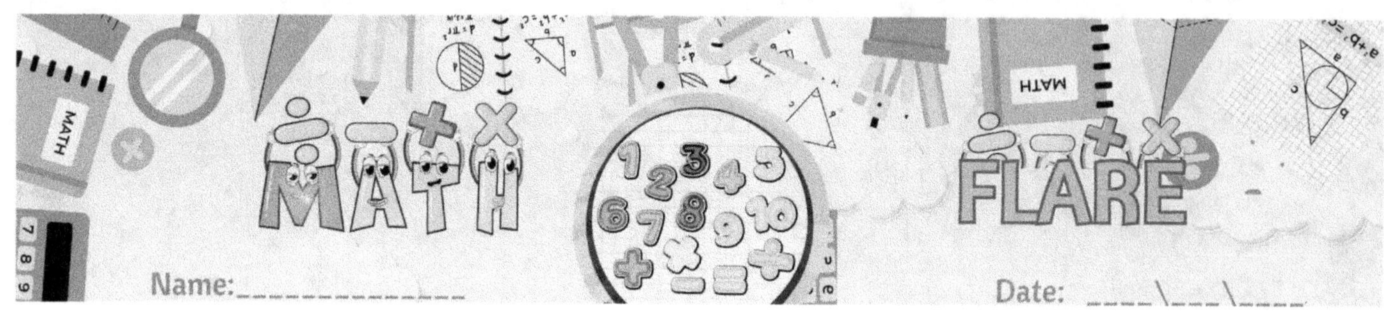

23. $2 = \dfrac{a}{2}$

24. $z + 2 = 8$

25. $1 = \dfrac{y}{1}$

26. $-1 = -4 + m$

27. $\dfrac{x}{2} = 3$

28. $-5 = -10 + z$

29. $\dfrac{x}{4} = 2$

30. $30 = 6x$

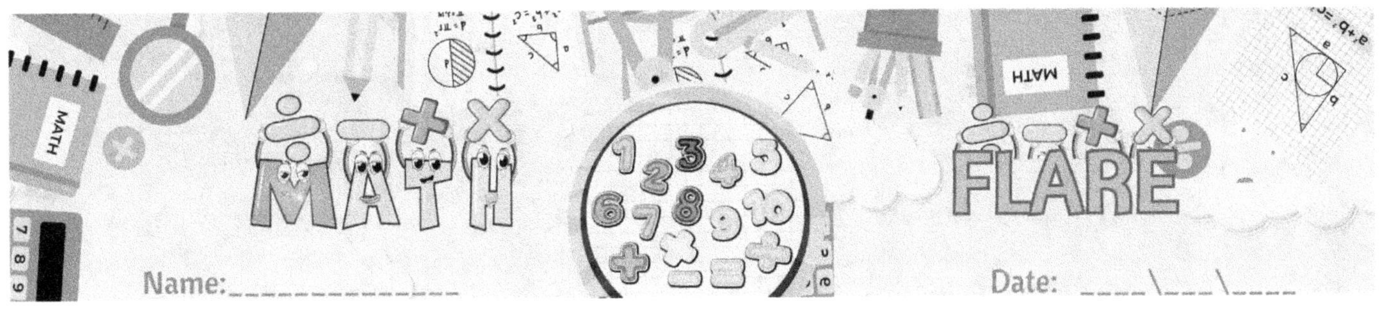

31. $a + 9 = 16$

32. $m - 2 = 3$

33. $-6 = x - 10$

34. $10s = 40$

35. $y - 7 = -4$

36. $-18 = -2z$

37. $7 = z - 2$

38. $\dfrac{m}{1} = 9$

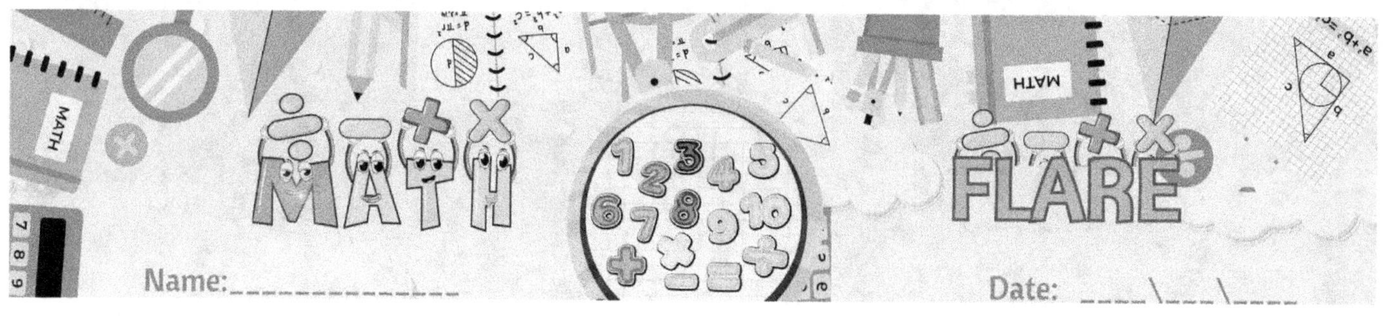

39. $\dfrac{x}{1} = 10$

40. $2 = \dfrac{z}{3}$

41. $-2 = b - 3$

42. $2 = \dfrac{z}{5}$

43. $2 = z$

44. $x + 1 = 9$

45. $-3 + x = -1$

46. $-15 = -5m$

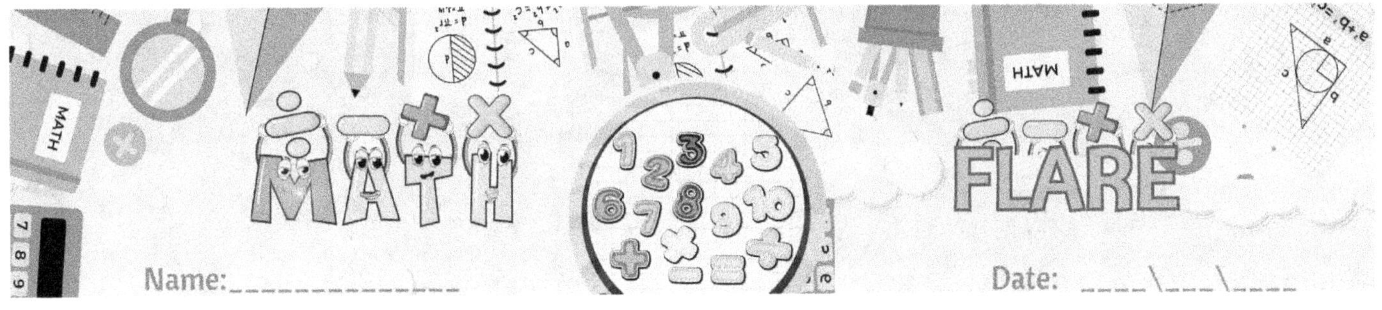

47. $-2 = x - 8$

48. $-12 = -6b$

49. $70 = 10a$

50. $-2 + x = 2$

51. $\dfrac{a}{2} = 5$

52. $8 = 2s$

53. $6 = z + 5$

54. $-5 + x = 1$

ANSWERS

Page 1: Place Value

1. 1 ten billion

2. 3 ten billions

3. 9 hundred thousands

4. 8 ten millions

5. 8 hundredths

6. 1 billion

7. 6 hundreds

8. 2 millions

9. 6 ten thousandths

10. 8 thousands

11. 5 thousandths

12. 2 billions

13. 4 ten millions

14. 4 ones

15. 4 tens

16. 8 ten thousandths

17. 5 tenths

18. 5 hundred millions

19. 1 ten

20. 7 hundred thousandths

21. 7 ones

22. 9 hundreds

23. 9 hundred thousands

24. 7 hundredths

25. 7 hundred millions

26. 2 hundred thousands

27. 3 millions

28. 7 hundredths

29. 3 hundredths

30. 0 hundred thousands

31. 0 tens

32. 1 million

33. 1 ten

34. 1 ten thousand

35. 8 hundredths

36. 2 ten millions

37. 5 hundredths

38. 7 tens

39. 5 ones

40. 7 thousands

41. 6 ten billions

42. 5 hundred thousands

43. 5 hundred thousands

44. 2 tens

45. 7 ten thousandths

46. 8 ten thousands

47. 9 ten millions

48. 5 hundreds

49. 8 hundredths

50. 8 ones

51. 6 millions

52. 2 tens

53. 8 hundredths

54. 4 hundreds

55. 6 tenths

Page 8: Operations with Whole Numbers

1. 8	2. -4	3. 8	4. 9	5. 7	6. 5	7. 5
8. 10	9. -2	10. 10	11. 9	12. 7	13. -17	14. -9
15. -7	16. -2	17. 4	18. -3	19. 8	20. 2	21. -13
22. -12	23. -8	24. 4	25. -4	26. 5	27. 12	28. 13
29. 0	30. 4	31. 8	32. 14	33. 7	34. -11	35. 13
36. -4	37. 2	38. -1	39. -1	40. -3	41. -4	42. 9
43. 4	44. -1	45. 4	46. -1	47. 4	48. -20	49. 5
50. -9	51. 0	52. -9	53. -1	54. 16	55. 0	56. 14
57. 7	58. 6	59. -2	60. 0	61. -17	62. 6	63. 6
64. 2	65. 5	66. 3	67. -9	68. -1	69. 9	70. -2

71. 12   72. 5   73. -1   74. -10   75. 4   76. -8   77. 9

78. 11   79. -13   80. -12   81. 5   82. 6   83. 1   84. -14

85. 6   86. -19   87. -5   88. 0   89. -8   90. 15   91. -10

92. 5   93. 4   94. -11   95. -3   96. 10   97. -12   98. -7

Page 18: Operations with Decimals

1. 14.35   2. 160.54   3. 20.58   4. 1.7   5. 10.40

6. 30.58   7. 2.4   8. 127.00   9. 44.24   10. 6.46

11. 3.54   12. 45.68   13. 0.6   14. 63.17   15. 71.91

16. 0.7   17. 1.3   18. 0.6   19. 18.04   20. 15.60

21. 9.35   22. 77.28   23. 55.43   24. 6.89   25. 122.66

26. 1.2   27. 1.9   28. 7.55   29. 81.02   30. 101.69

31. 18.59   32. 128.36   33. 72.58   34. 6.29   35. 9.62

36. 0.6   37. 26.97   38. 9.86   39. 139.56   40. 128.12

41. 50.00   42. 99.67   43. 105.69   44. 10.71   45. 1.1

46. 94.63   47. 18.65   48. 33.08   49. 13.20   50. 91.75

51. 7.72   52. 23.55   53. 22.27   54. 61.32   55. 38.27

56. 42.24   57. 1.9   58. 0.8   59. 12.61   60. 37.05

61. 0.8   62. 4.2   63. 63.42   64. 131.43   65. 30.60

66. 0.3   67. 0.36   68. 7.14   69. 120.92   70. 1.38

71. 24.96   72. 1.8   73. 133.73   74. 72.15   75. 0.5

76. 45.60   77. 157.76   78. 0.2   79. 33.98   80. 34.91

81. 15.13	82. 92.80	83. 49.46	84. 6.10	85. 31.96
86. 19.67	87. 20.28	88. 41.60	89. 19.72	90. 25.38
91. 1.0	92. 64.39	93. 130.97	94. 1.6	95. 158.39
96. 118.04	97. 2.08	98. 0.8	99. 24.00	100. 130.04
101. 38.34	102. 17.78	103. 121.80	104. 71.20	105. 25.75
106. 91.58	107. 13.99	108. 2.4	109. 12.78	110. 162.45
111. 67.89	112. 22.72	113. 0.7	114. 66.75	115. 80.82
116. 38.64	117. 10.27	118. 0.3	119. 63.69	120. 0.4
121. 26.59	122. 21.36	123. 101.87	124. 84.69	125. 150.75
126. 1.3	127. 6.5	128. 1.3	129. 0.5	130. 14.59
131. 40.95	132. 1.3	133. 61.56	134. 16.40	135. 161.07
136. 46.17	137. 6.80	138. 2.4	139. 152.74	140. 17.00
141. 119.23	142. 3.20	143. 146.60	144. 20.61	145. 1.6
146. 3.0	147. 23.66	148. 0.8	149. 62.69	150. 26.28
151. 81.88	152. 0.3	153. 0.6	154. 34.94	155. 57.36
156. 0.8	157. 9.52	158. 76.25	159. 62.79	160. 18.20
161. 0.3	162. 3.6	163. 1.6	164. 17.50	165. 60.48
166. 30.55	167. 11.66	168. 78.85	169. 108.90	170. 28.60
171. 25.16	172. 0.4	173. 114.02	174. 3.1	175. 124.60
176. 110.40	177. 108.46	178. 3.7	179. 130.58	180. 0.4
181. 1.0	182. 74.68	183. 1.1	184. 98.20	185. 9.88

186. 73.11 187. 72.67 188. 4.00 189. 1.1 190. 42.77

191. 1.3 192. 21.61 193. 17.13 194. 0.8 195. 1.6

196. 42.63 197. 39.50 198. 44.31 199. 26.56 200. 88.44

Page 31: Exponents

1. 225 2. 6,561 3. 121 4. 16 5. 1,000

6. 289 7. 1/1331 8. 2,744 9. 1/121 10. 104,976

11. 324 12. 1/125 13. 1/256 14. 1 15. 83,521

16. 1/64 17. 8 18. 1/9 19. 1,331 20. 1/2197

21. 1/4 22. 1/16 23. 1/729 24. 64 25. 1/8000

26. 6,859 27. 81 28. 1/3375 29. 1/144 30. 1/1728

31. 49 32. 1/216 33. 50,625 34. 1/8 35. 169

36. 130,321 37. 4,096 38. 1/100 39. 65,536 40. 27

41. 1 42. 400 43. 1/81 44. 343 45. 20,736

46. 1 47. 1/64 48. 125 49. 1/512 50. 1/4913

51. 16 52. 1/225 53. 1/6859 54. 25 55. 1

56. 8,000 57. 64 58. 256 59. 1/196 60. 1,728

Page 36: Square and Cube Roots

1. 7 2. 2 3. 6 4. 1 5. 2 6. 7 7. 9 8. 85

9. 12 10. 26 11. 18 12. 6 13. 22 14. 4 15. 10 16. 1

17. 2 18. 3 19. 5 20. 6 21. 15 22. 4 23. 15 24. 10

25. 5 26. 8 27. 7 28. 46 29. 8 30. 1 31. 28 32. 24

33. 61   34. 4   35. 43   36. 11   37. 59   38. 3   39. 19   40. 53

41. 54   42. 80   43. 9   44. 3   45. 9   46. 51   47. 57   48. 17

49. 76   50. 10   51. 58   52. 8   53. 37   54. 40   55. 19   56. 71

57. 14   58. 29   59. 63   60. 38   61. 42   62. 22   63. 31   64. 17

65. 77   66. 79   67. 5   68. 47

Page 41: Multiple Operations with Fractions

1. 1 3/8   2. 1 13/24   3. 2 2/5   4. 13/15

5. 89/120   6. 113/120   7. 4/5   8. 2 1/4

9. 11/14   10. 2   11. 1 17/84   12. 63/1000

13. 73/84   14. 1 7/60   15. 2 7/24   16. 7/8

17. 7/300   18. 2 5/24   19. 2 155/504   20. 5/14

21. 1 10/63   22. 1 1/12   23. 1 5/21   24. 169/280

25. 1 1/5   26. 1 227/360   27. 1 23/72   28. 1 71/84

29. 1 31/56   30. 1/160   31. 1/8   32. 1/12

33. 1/140   34. 1 19/42   35. 11/72   36. 2/45

37. 1 11/20   38. 11/12   39. 1 11/126   40. 49/72

Page 51: Convert: Ratio, Fraction, Percent, and Decimals

1.

	Ratio	Fraction	Percent	Decimal
a.	5:17	5/17	29.4%	0.294
b.	10:11	10/11	90.9%	0.909
c.	14:15	14/15	93.3%	0.933
d.	2:18	2/18	11.1%	0.111
e.	1:8	1/8	12.5%	0.125
f.	8:9	8/9	88.9%	0.889
g.	14:18	14/18	77.8%	0.778
h.	7:14	7/14	50%	0.5
i.	1:1	1/1	100%	1
j.	1:3	1/3	33.3%	0.333
k.	1:2	1/2	50%	0.5
l.	10:13	10/13	76.9%	0.769
m.	3:10	3/10	30%	0.3
n.	4:9	4/9	44.4%	0.444
o.	8:10	8/10	80%	0.8

2.

	Ratio	Fraction	Percent	Decimal
a.	4:4	4/4	100%	1
b.	5:15	5/15	33.3%	0.333
c.	5:19	5/19	26.3%	0.263
d.	3:13	3/13	23.1%	0.231
e.	7:17	7/17	41.2%	0.412
f.	4:18	4/18	22.2%	0.222
g.	2:16	2/16	12.5%	0.125
h.	9:19	9/19	47.4%	0.474
i.	5:12	5/12	41.7%	0.417
j.	11:13	11/13	84.6%	0.846
k.	4:9	4/9	44.4%	0.444
l.	4:19	4/19	21.1%	0.211
m.	9:12	9/12	75%	0.75
n.	2:14	2/14	14.3%	0.143
o.	8:9	8/9	88.9%	0.889

3.

	Ratio	Fraction	Percent	Decimal
a.	15:16	15/16	93.8%	0.938
b.	12:14	12/14	85.7%	0.857
c.	4:14	4/14	28.6%	0.286
d.	3:5	3/5	60%	0.6
e.	8:9	8/9	88.9%	0.889
f.	6:18	6/18	33.3%	0.333
g.	1:10	1/10	10%	0.1
h.	5:15	5/15	33.3%	0.333
i.	2:5	2/5	40%	0.4
j.	8:15	8/15	53.3%	0.533
k.	4:7	4/7	57.1%	0.571
l.	10:12	10/12	83.3%	0.833
m.	15:17	15/17	88.2%	0.882
n.	5:6	5/6	83.3%	0.833
o.	2:3	2/3	66.7%	0.667

4.

	Ratio	Fraction	Percent	Decimal
a.	2:14	2/14	14.3%	0.143
b.	3:4	3/4	75%	0.75
c.	5:14	5/14	35.7%	0.357
d.	12:12	12/12	100%	1
e.	2:6	2/6	33.3%	0.333
f.	6:10	6/10	60%	0.6
g.	8:19	8/19	42.1%	0.421
h.	13:19	13/19	68.4%	0.684
i.	4:15	4/15	26.7%	0.267
j.	1:3	1/3	33.3%	0.333
k.	4:13	4/13	30.8%	0.308
l.	4:10	4/10	40%	0.4
m.	4:5	4/5	80%	0.8
n.	7:14	7/14	50%	0.5
o.	6:14	6/14	42.9%	0.429

5.

	Ratio	Fraction	Percent	Decimal
a.	5:7	5/7	71.4%	0.714
b.	2:3	2/3	66.7%	0.667
c.	5:14	5/14	35.7%	0.357
d.	11:13	11/13	84.6%	0.846
e.	3:10	3/10	30%	0.3
f.	1:3	1/3	33.3%	0.333
g.	2:7	2/7	28.6%	0.286
h.	17:19	17/19	89.5%	0.895
i.	9:18	9/18	50%	0.5
j.	7:14	7/14	50%	0.5
k.	9:20	9/20	45%	0.45
l.	10:10	10/10	100%	1
m.	9:10	9/10	90%	0.9
n.	4:18	4/18	22.2%	0.222
o.	6:14	6/14	42.9%	0.429

Page 56: Solving One-Step Equations

1. 4   2. 5   3. 4   4. 3   5. 10   6. 7   7. 3   8. 1   9. 6

10. 5   11. 3   12. 6   13. 8   14. 6   15. 2   16. 3   17. 7   18. 4

19. 1   20. 3   21. 10   22. 5   23. 4   24. 6   25. 1   26. 3   27. 6

28. 5   29. 8   30. 5   31. 7   32. 5   33. 4   34. 4   35. 3   36. 9

37. 9   38. 9   39. 10   40. 6   41. 1   42. 10   43. 2   44. 8   45. 2

46. 3   47. 6   48. 2   49. 7   50. 4   51. 10   52. 4   53. 1   54. 6

www.ingramcontent.com/pod-product-compliance
Lightning Source LLC
Chambersburg PA
CBHW080941120726
48003CB00011B/3244